D0194861

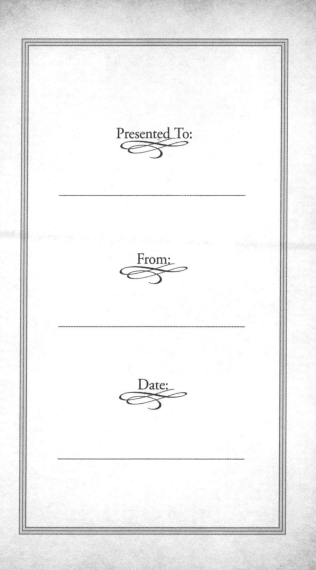

Presented To:

_____

From:

_____

Date:

_____

Destiny Image Books by Charles Slagle

*From the Father's Heart*
*Invitation to Friendship*
*Power to Soar*

# ABBA CALLING

*Hearing...*
*From the Father's Heart*
*Every Day of the Year*

Charles Slagle

DESTINY IMAGE® PUBLISHERS, INC.

P.O. Box 310, Shippensburg, PA 17257-0310

*"Promoting Inspired Lives."*

This book and all other Destiny Image, Revival Press, Mercy Place, Fresh Bread, Destiny Image Fiction, and Treasure House books are available at Christian bookstores and distributors worldwide.

For a U.S. bookstore nearest you, call 1-800-722-6774.

For more information on foreign distributors, call 717-532-3040.

Reach us on the Internet: www.destinyimage.com.

ISBN 13 TP: 978-0-7684-4137-6

ISBN 13 Ebook: 978-0-7684-8824-1

For Worldwide Distribution, Printed in the U.S.A.

1 2 3 4 5 6 7 8 / 16 15 14 13 12

# *Dedication*

I dedicate this book to all those who are seeking to know their Heavenly Abba or "Daddy."

To those who are lonely and hurting, those who feel they are simply rejects, misfits, "basket cases," I want you to know that I understand all those emotions, all those torments.

But most of all, I want you to know that there is a Heavenly Father who loves you and wants to share His life with you. I have been changed by that very Abba, as He has revealed His heart to mine.

I pray that as you read the messages in this book, His power and love will reach deeply within you and cause you to know that it is Abba calling—calling you to crawl into His lap, so to speak, and let Him pour His healing, transforming love into you.

# *Acknowledgments*

Almost thirty years ago as my wife, Paula, and I traveled across the country and around the world sharing the Gospel, Abba placed a treasured sister/friend/mentor in our lives. Her name was Carolyn Barnett, and she began to teach me how to really *hear* from the Heavenly Father.

Although I had grown up in a loving Christian home, the picture of God that had evolved in my life left much to be desired. On one hand I was taught that He was a God of love and compassion; on the other hand I somehow came to believe He was a taskmaster who could never be pleased.

And even though Paula and I were pouring our lives into ministry to others and seeing countless miracles of God's power released, I, myself, lived in fear and brokenness—always feeling that somehow, no matter how hard I tried, in the end God would turn His back on me, condemning me forever, without hope of reprieve.

When Carolyn realized the personal grief and torment at the core of my life, she began to encourage me to give God the opportunity to reveal Himself to me in a new and intimate way.

"Sit down and listen, Charles; quiet your heart, and then write down what you even *think* the Father might be saying to you," she encouraged. "Then give Him opportunity, and He will confirm that He really has spoken to you."

When I began to do that, giving Him opportunity to share what He was really like, my life began to change. The content of this book was born in just that way. From those times of quiet revelation, I began to understand our Heavenly Father in ways I had never imagined. I've yet to hear an audible voice, but again and again confirmation has come, letting me know that it really *was* Abba sharing His heart, His perspective, His love with me.

So before anything else is said or thanks offered to any others, I must thank Abba Father for His patience with me, His commitment to me, and His eagerness to share His heart. Apart from Him, this book would not exist.

Next, a huge debt of thanks and credit goes to all the folks at Destiny Image Publishers who worked on getting this book into your hands. The concept for this edition was birthed in their hearts. And without their persistent encouragement and tenacious support (and even gentle proddings, at times! ☺) this book never would have seen the printed page. It is an edited compilation of three separate books I have written and published with Destiny Image over the years—*From the Father's Heart, Volumes I & II* and *Power to Soar.*

From day one, Destiny has encouraged and supported me in sharing what Abba has poured into me. Their heart to see this edition released has been amazing. With anointed input from the editors and staff, the messages Father has given me over the years have been arranged into a format that offers a word from Abba each day of the year.

We applaud each of you at Destiny Image (and you each know to whom I speak) for your vision for this project and for the simple beauty of this volume, both inside and out. This book's design, format, and content are the result of much loving and meticulous input, labor, and care.

And no list of thanks would be complete without including my lovely wife, Paula. It has been her tireless support and many labors of love for the past forty-four years that have opened my eyes to our Father's truly unconditional love. I love you, Paula!

# Welcome

*Psalm 121;*
*Zephaniah 3:17;*
*Romans 8:31-39*

Child,

If anyone wants you to succeed, I do. If anyone is on your side, I AM. There is no one more committed to your happiness than I, and no one even begins to love you as I do. And I want to clarify something. My love for you is more—far more—than a patronizing concern for your welfare. I like you. I enjoy you.

I realize you find all this hard to believe, but I want you to believe it. You'll have to sooner or later, so why not now? I think about you all the time; and I will stop at nothing to remind you of My presence. Haven't you noticed?

Entreatingly,

Dad

Struggling Deliverer,

Next time, begin the day with authority. I gave you not a spirit of fear, but a spirit of love, power, and of self-management. Begin to act like it. Decide to keep a sense of humor. Laugh at all mistakes, interruptions, and obstacles, and stop worrying about your ignorance.

Actually, I AM in charge of your ignorance as well as your knowledge. Aren't you relieved? Think about it. Hasn't your mouth uttered deeper wisdom than you dreamed possible when you have simply been yourself, while oblivious to the tensions, the issues around you? Someone ignorant of all the rules can be a miracle-worker, and the knowledge of too many problems can create a prison. Remember that all belongs to Me, whether things revealed or things yet to appear. And *you* belong to Me.

Live in the joy of that fact. Thanks!

Always,

Abba

Tired Trooper,

Thank you for trusting and for not giving up. Yes, you yelped and squirmed a little. So what? You stood, stubbornly trusting My Word. That's what counts! Yes, you wavered for a moment—but have you noticed? Your lapses are growing farther apart. They are also shorter and less profound when they occur. Your progress delights Me!

Expect strength to surge within you as you go, trusting in Me. I can pack the benefits of twelve hours of sleep into two. No problem! Dare to arise, singing!

Today's revelation? Keep walking. I AM!

Yours joyfully,

Dad

Devoted Disciple,

As I have promised, you will see the King reigning in glory! You will recognize the true reign of Christ when His anointed co-regents no longer strive and quibble about words, but walk in the power of Kingdom love. When hurting people can look to one of His followers as a mighty rock providing cool shade and protection, or as a stream springing forth in a parched desert, the reign of My Son will then be self-evident—unmistakably obvious and undeniable.

Now do you see why I have been allowing you these opportunities to show patience and forgiveness? I have been answering your prayers. Do you remember? I do. You have repeatedly prayed for love, unity, and cooperation among the members of our house, and, naturally, I have begun the work in you. As you are discovering, no one is more dedicated to the principle of "first things first" than I.

Cheer up! Despite your doubts, you are progressing better than you think. And bear in mind that your brothers and sisters are undergoing the very same training throughout the world. As I have told you, the Church and the world are on the brink of an unprecedented wave of My glory and power. Right now, I AM preparing you and many others for mighty healing exploits that will bring great joy to people everywhere. Meanwhile, will you be patient with yourself? With others? And with Me? I AM!

Many thanks,

Dad

Unrelenting Warrior,

Tired minds need rest, not more information bombarding them! I have more—much more—to tell you. Many marvels, revelations, and gifts await your discovery. But first you must rest. Then you will receive them as blessings and not as burdens.

Refusing rest makes the mind vulnerable to vices. Seduction loves to entrap My trustworthy workers by whispering, "Break time!" I would weep seeing you broken.

I don't mind repeating—rest in My love! You will have to, sooner or later. Why not begin now?

Tenderly,

Dad

Fretful Freedom Fighter,

Shall I tell you about real joy? Joy begins by knowing Me and then is multiplied by taking an interest in people—not things, conditions, or acquisitions. And happiness never just happens. No, happiness is a result—a by-product. One feels it by receiving My love and joy and then giving them away. Happiness is a choice. A man or a woman must *decide* to be happy—now. Has it ever come to your mind that most unhappiness stems from ingratitude and failure to take pleasure in the gifts you already have?

Child, when will you learn to joy in the midst of all circumstances? If they be hard, delightful, or perhaps just suddenly different—lay hold of contentment and take joy as My gift! It is My gift, for contentment comes not by external conditions—it is the fruit of simply trusting in Me.

Again, happiness is a choice! So, in a very important sense, to choose happiness is to welcome the Kingdom of Heaven. Will you welcome it now? Be happy! Find reasons to rejoice and make opportunities to relieve the sufferings of others. Learn to be content in every circumstance—including this present one. Begin now to enjoy and advance our Kingdom by giving thanks. Your joy will overflow, I promise.

By the way, you are obviously right about one thing—I have not answered some of your prayers, for I have deliberately ignored your pleas that I shorten your earthly days and immediately transfer you to Heaven. And you should be grateful that I have. Honestly, child. You had no idea what you were asking. I mean, in your recent frame of mind your presence here would hardly have proven a blessing to you—or to any of the rest of us, for that matter!

Truly but tenderly,

Dad

Sorrowful Child,

So you want revenge, do you? Good luck! You'll need all the luck you can get without God.

I know. You sought counsel and received condemning judgment instead. People scorned your weakness and exploited your pain. Foolish mortals! Pray for them, child. Your betrayers must learn mercy the hard way. I promise you, they will learn.

Forgiveness is an act of the will. My will inclines toward forgiveness. Aren't you grateful? Then please align your will with Mine. No pressure. I will help you. I love you too much to hold grudges.

All I ask is that you choose to forgive, and I will help you forget. You're doing your part. Thank you for trusting while I'm doing Mine. You will not always suffer this pain. Thank you for yielding your rights to Me. Aren't you glad there's nothing left to violate?

With deepest compassion and respect,

Abba

Delightful Deliverer!

You are not wrong to be stepping out in faith at the moment. After all, I AM the One who released you into this path by My very own words, am I not? Just remember not to judge by outward appearances. Also, refuse to retreat into doubt and introspection when some of those little steps you are taking seem to fall short of shaking Heaven and earth. Bear in mind—it is first the seed and the sprout, then the stalk and the foliage, and finally the flower and the fruit.

Treasured child, our Kingdom is an enduring one. It is built on a Solid Foundation. Our Kingdom is a quiet one, but an invincible one. It expands slowly, scarcely noticed, as I cause it to grow. One day it will fill all the earth! Is it noise and fireworks you want, or power?

I have spoken these thoughts to your heart already, but I knew you would enjoy having them confirmed. Keep moving! I AM!

Proudly! Joyfully!

Dad

# Day 8

*Joshua 2; Matthew 21:31;*
*Luke 10:25-37; John 8:2-11*

Learning Liberator,

Two Bible teachers eased their sedans around the blazing di-saster and drove on to their "ministry" appointments. Moments later, a male prostitute abandoned his motorbike and braved the flames to pry a screaming toddler from the wreckage. Which of these three men would you call righteous?

I would rather live with fornicators than fault-finders. Forni-cators are addicted to pleasure, and pain results as a by-product. Fault-finders find pleasure in hurting despairing hearts—will-fully! Pleasure addicts are easier to cure than chronic accusers. One accuser became a devil, do you recall?

I often employ unexpected, even disreputable-looking sources to nurture My prophets and miracle-workers. Ravens, not doves, fed Elijah. A prostitute once provided shelter for two men I had commissioned. Do you want to impress fickle minds or to work miracles?

Thanks for listening,

Dad

# Day 9

Fearful One,

You have My Word; what else do you need? Have I ever betrayed or forsaken you? Jesus promised, *"...the one who comes to Me I will by no means cast out,"* did He not? Then you must choose to remember His promise and decide to forget your doubts. Now—more than ever—trust is a must. So will you forsake those fears and refuse to heed outward appearances? Sooner or later you must, for despite your doubts or those of anyone else, I AM at work to fulfill My words.

Trust Me now! If you will, this test need not come again. These things were allowed, not to decrease your faith, but to enlarge it. I AM answering your prayers that I enlarge your heart to contain greater faith. And I have used the debased and the weak to do it—even the frailty of your own flesh.

Never fear, I will keep every promise. Meanwhile, will you trust My integrity to hold you up by grace? That kind of trust builds the foundation for all victories to follow, and it is the only commitment I ask of you. I will fulfill My commitment; but now I AM enabling you to see that, by My grace, you also can fulfill yours. Trust Me. Can you think of a better plan of action? Not if it's My power you want.

Forever!

Dad

*Matthew 7:9-11;*
*Psalm 118:24*

Needy Child,

I have prepared this day for your pleasure, believe it or not. Ask and you shall receive! Seek and you will find!

Since you don't give a hoot about who gets the best slice of turf, I AM giving you the whole territory. Oceans, continents, polar regions, forests, islands, mineral rights, mountain ranges. And best of all, with Christ, you will inherit and bless the nations! How does it feel to be rich?

Why do you feel guilty about asking Me for extras and not just necessities? When your heart priorities align with My loving purposes, I delight in fulfilling the most fleeting desires of My children. Do you require your children to live on weeds, worms, and water? Existence is possible on such fare, you know.

Why do you keep looking in your mailbox? Supply will arrive soon—I am delighted to do it, child. You can trust My reliability; just don't expect predictability.

Your grateful heart delights Me!

Yours forever,

Dad

# Day 11

*First Kings 19:11-12;*
*Matthew 13:15-17*

Truth Seeker,

It is just not My style to thunder from Heaven with a booming voice accompanied by the special effects of wind and fire—not usually, anyway. No, I have purposely planned to speak softly so those who truly yearn to hear My voice will hear it—but only those. Furthermore, it is not My nature to intrude where I AM not wanted! And being the very Author of protocol and propriety, I seldom have done so, except in rare moments when expediency required it for the sake of all. Besides (though some will never believe it), I usually prefer a subtle and more natural approach to the obviously supernatural.

I do speak, and I speak more often than you imagine, but all who want to hear Me must listen. All have spiritual ears. I have seen to that. However, at present very few in your world even think about them, let alone choose to use them! Do you remember that Jesus said of the clergy of His day, "they have ears, but will not hear with them"? Child, hearing is a choice! It is just that simple.

I know that you really want to converse with Me. So decide now to listen to the words that My Spirit whispers in your deepest being. Then dare to respond to them! Trust My Spirit to guide you and protect you and refuse to yield to the clamor of your emotions. Laugh in the face of fear and worry will flee from you! Remember, I AM with you. Adventure awaits us. Let's enjoy real relationship.

Yours with all power,

Abba

Broken One,

I have not betrayed you. Mortals have, I know. But may I share a secret with you? At this very moment—even now—you hold great power either of life or death, sorrow or loss in your hands. I AM not often angry, yet today I AM for the pain they willfully caused you.

Thank you for allowing Me to defend your interests! I AM happy you asked Me to do so. Yes, vengeance is Mine! I will repay. So what would you have Me to do? Search your heart, and do consider very carefully, for what is done cannot be undone, little one.

Shall I judge them strictly by the ways they have dealt with you? Or shall I consider all preceding factors—their shattered hopes, their inner struggles—even as I have done for you? And what if they repent? You decide. I await your answer patiently, sorrowfully, and with deepest compassion.

Tenderly,

Dad

P.S. I trust you. Remember, mercy triumphs over judgment!

*Psalm 34:1-10*

Bold Pioneer!

You have come this far, so what makes you think you will fall short of the goal now? Have you been listening to all those "wise reasoners" again? You know—those who delight in foreseeing problems, criticizing failures, and freely voicing their opinions while dwelling in the comfortable safety of theory, unbelief, and inactivity?

Words, words, and more worthless words! When will you finally decide to believe in the gifts I placed within you and choose to laugh at all those silly reasonings?

If it is safety you want, then you will do far better to listen to Me and follow your heart. Hasn't experience already shown you this? You know it has. Besides, pioneers like ourselves have always seen safety in a different light than those who try to make a career out of it; don't you agree? Laugh at the threats, child. Laugh and get on with enjoying your life! I do. Follow your heart and follow your dream! I AM with you, so what else do you think you will ever need? A few more prophets of gloom and doom? Not on your life! And certainly not on Mine.

Still chuckling,

Dad

*Philippians 3:12-15;*
*Second Timothy 2:13;*
*First John 1:9*

Self-scrutinizing One,

Unless I lead you to do so, looking back hurts far more than it helps. Avoid the snare of morbid introspection! I have redeemed your yesterdays and will guard your tomorrows. I will heal the wounds of your heart.

Again, child, will you trust Me? I delight in turning blunders into blessings for the yielded and humble of heart. You cannot defeat My power by dwelling in the past. You only delay—to your own pain—the manifestation of its full glory.

Instead of making rash vows, just remember My vows to you. Heaven celebrates your progress! Forget the past. Rejoice in My love. Focus on now—and be happy! Heaven desires it. I command it. You deserve it!

With deepest compassion,

Abba

Beloved Child,

   Again, any seeming "message from God" that destroys hope simply is not from Me. It is in light of this obvious truth, treasured child, that you must test all things and cling to that which is good. I will help you.

Always,

Dad

# Day 16

Weary One,

When I ask you to sing praises and to delight in Me from your heart, please bear in mind—I AM not seeking your encouragement. Since when did Everlasting Strength need encouragement? Or anything else for that matter?

My command to give praise is a love command. I AM inviting you to join the Dance—the Cosmic Celebration of Joy! There and there alone can you learn the Song of songs. And there only can you also hear the song I have sung over you since you were born.

Enter My courts! Come into them—with praise! Praise is the gateway to My throne room. So praise, child! Enter in by praise! I AM drawing you into the melody all Heaven has been singing since before time began. We have a glorious song to sing, you and I, and the tedious drone of earth-songs will disappear in the splendor of ours, I assure you.

And when you sing our song, hurting one, our hearts will harmonize as one. In the glory of that union all else will harmonize as well. But you must sing the Song of praise so that you may truly see.

Your Dad

Dear Child,

Reality exterminates myths. By its very nature, truth scoffs at trivia by showing it up as the sham that it is. Child, do you expect to reflect My Light and live free of flak at the same time? Jesus couldn't!

Yours with deepest understanding,

Abba

Weary One,

Of course not! It doesn't anger Me when you grow weary of dealing with people. I understand when you become exhausted from smiling, nodding, listening. Bone-tired of talking, talking, talking! Your brain needs rest because it, too, is a part of your body. Shouldn't I know?

On occasion I lead you into the company of the stubborn, the opinionated, and the adamant. Sometimes you need a refresher course that reminds you of what not to become.

Slip behind the door and join Me for a chuckle when anyone nitpicks with your anointing and calling. When you need adjustment, I will see to it, child. Haven't I always?

Thank you for lavishing love and grace upon the undeserving and the ungrateful. That's what life is all about, isn't it?

Thank you for trusting,

Dad

Zealous Child,

An explosion waiting to happen; "hell on wheels" some people called you. Yet I won your heart with My tenderness, didn't I? What do you mean you want Me to teach them a lesson? Hmmm...

Dad

# Day 20

Chosen Conqueror,

Comparison is simply asking for depression. No one is *literally* equal to anyone else because I have created the human family in such a way as to foster mutual need and a supportive sharing among its members. You may as well learn to live with this fact: you will never be equal to your friends or even your enemies, because I never intended that you be.

Frankly, the whole idea of equality is a fallacy, for no real person ever could or ever should be an exact replica of another. If I had wanted tin soldiers, could I not have made them easily enough? But if I had, your very capacity to recognize inequality would not exist. You would not be a person at all, but only an empty copy of a concept, without the ability to be truly happy or unhappy. The "you" who now thinks to question My fairness would not even be. Has it never occurred to you that all sameness is equal—but equal to nothingness? To reduce all to the identical is to erase all potential for personhood and merely to arrange a new form of the trivial at best, and nothingness at worst. Is this the fate you would assign to yourself? Or all others?

Child, no two people can ever be equally interesting, conversant, intelligent, talented, or strong, for all have different needs and all have different gifts. And why? Because all were made to fit together as living stones comprising My Holy Temple—some large, some small, some short, some tall, some hard, some soft, but all for the glory of all.

Can you now see the futility of envy? Child, you have not because you ask not. Ask! I will complete you, but by association, not duplication. And believe it or not, I have wanted to complete others by introducing them to you! You do have many strengths you have forgotten in the midst of all your comparisons. So why not think of someone else for a change? If you will, I believe you will find yourself even liking yourself—in spite of yourself!

Patiently,

Dad

P.S. Remember, to complain and compare is to live in despair. How could one person's weakness ever rival another person's strength? It's as logical as two plus two equals five!

Child,

   Your heart is in the right place, so you are on the right track. True, some of your back-steps, side-steps, and sudden lurches make for an interesting...dance? But I love it. You're learning!

Proudly,

Dad

Diligent Disciple,

I AM not ashamed of you. You have embarrassed yourself, but you have not embarrassed Me. Not in the least.

I give you time to learn and space to grow because, as a wise Father, I know your welfare depends on your having actual knowledge, born of experience. Those who speak otherwise—saying My holiness demands instant perfection and flawless performance—know nothing of fatherhood and misrepresent Me in their ignorance.

My ways are not the ways of men. I AM not one to worry about outward appearances, and neither do I fret over the blunders of My children. I look at the heart. Don't you remember? I see all. In fact, I can see no other way. *All* is all I ever see. So how can One who sees everything at all times ever worry about anything at any time?

I thought you'd enjoy the reminder.

Love,

Dad

*Ephesians 4:1-6*

Racing Restorer,

Remember! I work over all, through all, and in all. When you slam doors and mutter and stomp, who are you raging against? Don't plunge into guilt. Just stop!

Please,

Abba

# Day 24

Child,

Being safe is hardly a worthwhile goal to seek. I mean, safety should be one of the very least concerns of a conqueror. How unlike you! Since when have you ever been one to worry about trying something different? So why are you beginning to play the cautious role at this stage of the game?

Shall I repeat some of your own advice to you? Come now! It was you who said, and you have said it repeatedly, "There is no safety apart from doing the Father's will." And again, you have also said, "The only thing that assures safety or protection of the truest quality is to follow Christ."

Child, you know I AM not one to nag or harass, so I will not belabor the point. But don't you think it's time to rid yourself of those ridiculous rehearsals for retreat? Repent! Let us enjoy a good laugh together!

Dad

Tender One,

Do you think I would admonish fathers not to browbeat their children and yet live contrary to My own counsel? Test the spirits! My Spirit never shackles people to shame.

Love,

Dad

Exhausted Seeker,

I enjoy your company more than you know. Not many of My children keep Me laughing the way you do. You may enjoy My company whenever you wish. Anywhere, any night or day, any moment!

Nothing about you ever bores Me. Not one bit. Your voice, your manner, your compassionate heart—everything about you I find intriguing, unique, and delightful. I find nothing more boring than the religious lie that you must strive to earn My acceptance!

I just want to remind you that I AM here if you ever need a shoulder to cry on. And you needn't shout across light-years of ever-expanding cosmos to reach Me. Why reach for what you already have? Bask in the serenity of My Presence. Stop analyzing past conversations and fretting about possible conflicts. I have you covered!

Whatever else you may forget, never forget this: I love you too much to lose you! I AM thinking of you. Let's enjoy one another.

Everlastingly yours,

Dad

Cherished Child,

No one can buy you! You are far too costly. *By His cross*, your Lord affirmed you as My child, giving you a value that defies all computation! Return all gifts that arrive with strings attached. Quickly! Post haste! Yesterday!

Always your Ally,

Dad

# Day 28

Anxious One,

You do have favor. You have Mine. You are radiant, filled and surrounded with My glory! And although My glory may not always feel very glorious to your emotions or appear very glorious to your natural eyes, it abides with you nevertheless. It is an invisible shield; like any other shield, its worth is determined by what it does, not by how it appears.

Have I not recently shown you the power of My Presence that surrounds you? You know I have. I have granted you favor in the marketplace where you least expected it. I have opened doors no one else ever could have opened. I have protected you from losses you never could have foreseen given a million lifetimes. And gladly have I done it!

Child, I don't mind your having grown accustomed to My glory, and neither am I offended that you have learned to walk in it with hardly a thought of its presence. Would you expect your own children to be constantly thanking you for the roof over their heads or the clothes on their backs? Of course not!

And so it is with Me, anointed one. My glory is your natural inheritance! I was just wondering why you have been entertaining all those irrational fears lately—pleading for My protection and favor when you've had them all this time.

Tenderly,

Dad

Deliberating One,

Are you sure this is what you want? At some point I would enjoy seeing you do something you actually like.

Take courage! My thoughts are now your thoughts. So, your thoughts (ordinary as they may feel) are indeed coming from Me. Enjoy exploits!

Powerfully yours,

Abba

Delightful Child,

There is just no way to avoid some of those long stretches of "silence," as you call them. As your own experience has proven, My plans for you far exceed your ability to imagine.

What use is information to a man ravaged by the ache of physical need? Would giving him a course in human psychology or anatomy satisfy his hunger, quench his thirst, or relieve his pain? So it is with you, child. Now is a feeding time, a building time— not a time for words. When words are needed I will speak them; you know I always have.

For now, will you review those words I spoke to you earlier? If you will, I think you'll find your questions already answered. And never mind the apologies. You've not disillusioned Me. How could you? I never had any illusions.

And what makes you think I have given up on you? That nonsense never crosses My mind except when you bring it up yourself. Has it ever occurred to you how your even thinking I would cuts Me to the heart? Child, your reluctance to trust My integrity hurts far more than any sin arising from the weakness of your flesh.

One day when you truly know Me and realize how much I care for you, you will also discover My strength has swallowed up your weakness.

Forever in joy!

Your Dad

Trusted Warrior,

My heart is aching. Do you mind if I cry on your shoulder for a few moments? I know this would sound silly to many people. Intercession attracts few in Our Household.

Thank you for caring,

Abba

Exasperated Warrior,

Yes, you exploded and unloaded. I saw the pressure mounting in you long before you discovered it. Nearly everyone wants a God of grace for themselves, yet they demand a God of wrath for others! Child, where do you stand on this issue?

You have seen the hypocrisy of human justice. Will you now trust Me to restore your losses? I've trusted you to endure a season of suffering, because I AM sensitizing your heart to heal shattered people.

Yes, I AM a God of exacting virtue and judgment, but above all else, I delight in mercy and kindness. And I enjoy being that way! So few understand My nature.

I love you too much to let those who victimize you live with no regrets. Stand still and behold My deliverance! This battle is not yours, but Mine. Keep rejoicing, and allow everyone to see My gentle mercy in you. I AM near. Refuse to worry! Express your every need to Me with thankfulness, cherished one. Peace that transcends earthly reason is yours for the receiving.

All is forgiven. Let's enjoy fresh beginnings.

Compassionately,

Dad

Grieving Child,

Just a gentle reminder...

David refused to retaliate against King Saul's abuse, yet he did dodge the spears his oppressor hurled at him! One can love from a distance if necessary. Trust Me to lead you. I plan wonderful refreshment for you. It is time for you to enjoy it.

With deepest compassion,

Abba

Little One,

Do you really believe I have burdened you with this inner conflict? Am I so cruel, so unreasonable? How could Love commit such an act? No, you know it isn't true. I AM the One who has been holding you, keeping you from utter despair in those hours you wept alone. I have seen your tears and I have known how you have yearned to please Me. I have cried with you, feeling the shame of your humiliation as if it were My own. And it was My own, little one, it was.

I have also noted the withdrawals and "righteous" judgments of those you trusted. Be assured, I saw it all. I have seen your desperate search for answers. When your pain drove you to share those secret sorrows of your heart, and they rewarded your trust with treachery, I stood with you. I know. They justified it all in My name and called it "honoring the Word" and "faithfulness to the cause of Christ," but may I tell you what I called it? I called it disgusting. Of all sins, from robbery to prostitution, I find none more revolting than sanctimony and hypocrisy. And there are certainly none more wicked.

Please. Will you remember that if foolish men judge by the outward appearance, it is not so with Me? I see the inner wounds beneath those surface sins the hypocrites love to gossip about—truly I do. Have I ever been One to snuff out a smoldering wick or trample a soul who is down? Come now! You know better. I AM the Righteous Judge.

So child, despite the failures of insecure people, will you please keep trusting in Me? Will you forgive them so the weight of their sins may be lifted from your tired shoulders? Heaven knows you've carried burdens enough.

And don't give up. Few others have known or cared, but I know how long you have waited. Your liberation is coming soon, sooner than you think, child! Sorrow not. Embrace joy—now! Even now the old is giving way to the new. Follow Me, and you will see!

Yours with everlasting commitment,

Abba

Frustrated Seeker,

So you think I always get My own way, do you? I've noticed it hasn't hampered you much. Count your blessings!

You're absolutely right. I do as I please, and nothing can stop Me! Isn't it wonderful to know that My loving heart governs all of My actions? Thank you for trusting.

Love,

Abba God

Matthew 23:1-12;
Ephesians 6:7-8;
First Peter 4:8-10

Striving Child,

Do you want to succeed in religion? Compete! Compare! Contrive an attractive public image and always maintain it. Cater to the rich, to the powerful. Never be seen with "losers." Crave human applause. Demand respect! If need be, slander and trample others to get it. And, at all costs, avoid Reality. Right? Wrong, actually!

When will you abandon the practice of observing appearances and seek supernatural insight? Your quest for the supernatural— why should it offend Me? I created you to yearn for My power. Lust for power to promote self, and despair will devour your dreams. Pursue Love, and you will perform exploits with Me!

I don't mind you expecting some recognition, little one. You deserve it! It is only natural that you should desire it. But why do you want recognition, and from whom? That is My question. Your happiness hinges on your answer.

I've ordained today's challenges to nudge you toward such revelation. Adventure awaits us. Let's enjoy!

Helpfully,

Dad

Delightful Child,

I love bragging about you in front of your fellow workers and friends! How can you get Me to stop? Simple enough. Just start singing your own praises, and I'll clam up immediately.

Yours cheerfully,

Dad

Diligent One,

Having done all you can do, refuse to take responsibility for the failures of others. Reject all temptation to introspect and stop analyzing your past. When I see you, I see you not as you were then, or even as you are now. No, I see the real you—the glorious you that, even now, I AM opening your own eyes to see!

Assuming guilt for the sins of others or for your own already forgiven sins only darkens the eyes of your spirit, tying you to problems not your own. Renounce the works of darkness! Refuse to rehearse their memories! Return to joy! I have all power and all things are in My control. Rejoice in My empowering grace!

You need not worry about "using" My grace. As I have said before, if you were to become lax or careless about it, I would be the first to let you know. Grace alone has power to save, child! If you don't use it, what else in earth or Heaven do you expect to use? Willpower? Positive thinking? Ha! I'm laughing with you—honestly.

Love,

Dad

*Ephesians 2:4-7;*
*Philippians 3:2,15*

Striving Child,

Scrub, polish, alter, whack, and chisel on your personality all you wish! Only My love can birth healing and holiness. My Son suffered untold agony to enthrone you in the highest of all positions. Why do you keep putting yourself down?

Respectfully,

Abba

Fretful One,

Don't look at the pain. Look at the plan! Look at the purpose! Why do you equate discipline with punishment? Why should I punish you? You are the one doing the punishing, not I. Do you expect Me to help you worsen the wound? Sorry. You're looking in the wrong department. If it's guilt and condemnation you want, you need to consult a good religionist—there is the place to look. But why not take My advice—have a good laugh and stay with the program?

Did you forget? I told you earlier that you would soon be in training for the big game of the season. Well, this is it! Rejoice and be glad! I know you. You can do it! By the way, have you had a good look at those muscles of yours lately? I have.

Proudly!

Dad

Daring Deliverer,

But of course! Often you will be misunderstood! It was the same with Jesus, do you recall? Yes, your Savior was constantly criticized for His unorthodox behavior.

When He showed courage, His critics called Him proud, and when love compelled Him to heal the sick on the Sabbath, contrary to religious custom, they accused Him of sin. Though Jesus was the very personification of humility, some thought Him dangerous. His acceptance of all people, without regard to their social standing often earned him contempt, not admiration.

And your Lord stirred up controversy constantly, just by virtue of what He was! Some thought Him too strict, while others thought Him too lenient. Still others labeled Him as a rebel, while many thought Him a pacifist. Do you recall how your Savior was often interrupted in the midst of His ministry? Rudely interrogated and mocked? I do. Yes, Jesus, the Lord of Glory, became the Object of ridicule, controversy, and gossip.

But He laughed the shame to scorn! And why? Jesus came to heal, not to please, and I delighted in His willing obedience. He revealed My true heart as no one else has ever done. Your Lord brought healing to multitudes. Yet despite all His amazing works, He could not satisfy all expectations. And neither can you! Nor do I even want you to! Are you relieved?

With deepest understanding,

Dad

*Philippians 2:5-11*

Frustrated Servant,

Child, I know you're tired of the trivia, but how many times do you think Jesus answered the same quibbling questions in a single day? Did people ever try to use Him for their own selfish ends? How slow were His disciples to comprehend His message? How often did the King of kings find Himself settling silly squabbles among His followers? Did those who demanded His time value it? Did Jesus ever meet with suspicion, unrealistic expectations, or ingratitude? Is the student greater than the Teacher? You decide.

My Beloved Son gladly came to serve, rather than to be served. His kind of ministry does demand His kind of cross. And child, it is merely your reasonable service. Remember, it is for the joy set before you. Joy, joy, and more joy, multiplied in this life and in the ages to come! And, yes, with some persecutions—but why not? After all, you are in very good Company.

Always by your side,

Dad

Fleeing Child,

Planning an excursion? I understand. You can leave Me if you want to. At least, you can try. Where will you go?

I'm not worried. You'll come back. But when you do, you will come without religion's burden of frantic self-effort and shame. Soon you'll laugh at any lying illusion that lures you to leave Me. Aren't you beginning to realize that I've made certain you'd find nothing to go back to?

Binges explode with a vengeance in the absence of joy, always! Better the pleasure of sin than no pleasure at all, right? Not really. Better to pause along the way to enjoy My flowers.

Yes, I'm glad you realize it now. When you rage against Me, you are only hurting yourself. Mad? Why should I be mad? You gave up for a moment, but I didn't. Nothing has changed between us. Will you believe Me? I want you to rest. I want you to know the Real Me. Soon you will!

Yours with commitment,

Abba

Cherished Child,

Has it ever come to your mind that I like ordinary things? Yes, the things you call ordinary are the very instruments I have chosen to use in your world, and I call them wonderful. They are just as miraculous as any other miracles I have—so please stop questioning your gifts, will you? Do we always have to be pulling rabbits out of hats?

What good is it to raise the dead and heal the sick if no one thinks to feed and clothe them after they have been raised and healed? Can't a man bearing a cup of cold water bring as timely a gift as any prophet? I think so.

Oh yes, I suppose My angels could supernaturally transport you from place to place all the time, but be honest! Would you not begin to miss using those marvelous miracles called "legs" after a while? "Holy Ghost" does not mean hocus pocus. Believe Me, I know Him better than anyone else.

So will you please stop worrying about having a ministry of miracles? Walk on with Me, keep walking in love, and give what you have to give. Miracles will happen, never fear. In fact, you will find them happening all the time!

Helpfully,

Dad

# Day 45

Matthew 26:6-13;
Luke 7:36-50;
Hebrews 12:2-3; 13:14-16

Weeping Worker,

Be at peace. Those who size you up and try to stuff you in a slot labeled "sinner" will come to their senses. I will see to that. Jesus endured slander, do you recall? But He laughed the shame to scorn. You do the same. I AM with you.

One can never do enough to satisfy a nit-picker! Some people, who have yet to reach the end of themselves, just seem to prefer the illusion of control. They have yet to discover True Happiness. Not so with you!

When you know you've done your very best, don't allow carping critics to destroy your joy. Trust Me to call all nit-pickers to task. I will!

Joyfully always,

Abba

Restless Truth Seeker,

The reason I sometimes refuse to inform you is so that I may direct you. Very often information can be a greater hindrance to ministering in the power of My Spirit than you realize. I mean, if at this stage I were to tell you more, you would tend to organize your life in such a way so as to bypass the creative ability of My anointing.

My truth is a living and active substance! It just cannot be reduced to mere words, formulas or formats. That is why it has the power to liberate! Don't you remember? The letter kills, but My Spirit gives life; My Spirit and My anointing are one and the same. In fact, My anointing is the very substance and essence of life itself! This being true, your words will have power only as they become the vehicles or the channels of My life-giving Spirit.

And herein lies the problem. Given too much advance notice, some of My more active communicators tend to elaborate upon words, plans, and concepts so the reality is often lost in the midst of its belabored description. The shadow then supplants the substance and prophecy dwindles to mere poetry. Reality recedes into rhetoric and truth disintegrates into theory, leaving hurting, empty people.

Now do you understand? Too much smoothness smothers and stifles, child. A stumbling sincerity and spontaneity are actually two of My favorite vehicles; but surely you've noticed by now? Keep up the good work! You are doing better than you think—at least from My point of view you are.

Proudly,

Dad

Disillusioned Disciple,

Spare yourself heartache. Don't demand perfection from people. Instead, expect daily reminders of My Presence and love. You will have them.

No one could live with you if you appeared too perfect in your own sight. Not even I could live with you, child. My glory best reveals itself through rough-hewn humanity, which Scripture calls "vessels of clay." Has it occurred to you that you just may qualify?

Aren't you glad I look beyond your behavior, beholding your pain and your weakness? All I ask is that you do the same for others. I will help you.

Yours cheerfully,

Abba

Chosen Liberator,

Despite your doubts, I AM at work. As I told you before, I AM preparing a place for you, and very soon you will know beyond all doubt who you really are and why you were destined to be. Why are you troubled at heart? My callings can never be cancelled, so be at peace about your qualifications, child. I AM.

Your gift will make room for itself and your own self as well; you will see! In fact, you will soon be seeing all things with new eyes from your new position of power and authority. Although you doubt and question, I AM yet committed to honor the deeper faith of your heart—the faith of My Son within you.

You apparently forgot, but it is His faith you are living by, is it not?

Proudly promoting you, I AM!

Abba

Delightful Deliverer,

When your authority or your validity is questioned, rejoice! Refuse to retreat—even for a moment.

Can't you see that the whole strategy behind the enemy's challenge is to convince you to question your commission and to retreat? Child, "retreat" and "defeat" are alien to Heavenly policy! They are words foreign to Kingdom language.

Have you forgotten? Great challenges often follow great conquests. This happened even in your Savior's ministry. His deeds and His words were often followed by the question, "By what authority does He do these things?" Yes, I knew you would recognize the familiar ring of those words. Be encouraged! Just think of it all as being a "part of the package." I do.

Gladly!

Abba

P.S. If you think about it, the lack of flak should be the occasion for questions. Don't you agree?

Sulking Restorer,

Are you angry with Me? Why? Because I neglected to solicit your opinion concerning My plans? And after all the times you've thanked Me for revising yours! Surely you're not serious!

I know you're going to like My plans. Allow Me the pleasure of popping up with a few surprises. Do you mind? You've asked Me to keep you flexible. I AM doing My best to accommodate.

Yours chuckling,

Almighty God

# Day 51

Matthew 7:11;
John 14:7; First John 4:18

Frantic Child,

These days you often hear that I AM a God of judgment, and it is true. I AM. Yet how could I be a loving Father of sound judgment and always be sneaking around looking for reasons to reject My own children? Would a sensible earthly father do this? Think about it.

If you spent more time with Me and less with those who merely enjoy talking about Me, I know you would be far happier. Has it come to your mind that all of us might be happier if you were? Child, your fear of failure does tend to put everyone else on edge, so the time has come to lay those fears to rest, once and for all. Come, let us reason together!

How can anyone who knows anything about Jesus (who perfectly reflected My nature) portray Me as spiteful and ill-tempered? That fault-finding god of hard-line religion may be many things, but he could never be Jesus or Me. Can you imagine such a neurotic, pompous deity dying for his creatures? Hardly. A god so devoid of common decency and good sense could neither love nor give, and he certainly would lack the ability to create anything.

Child, that silly god-version could not so much as create a molecule, let alone sustain a universe! No, he could only be what he is—a pitiful projection of fear and guilt, a phantom haunting the hearts of men who think they must scramble to save themselves by earning My love. Such ones have yet to see that "salvation by grace through faith" literally means "trusting Me to free them by love, not merit." My heart aches for them, for they have yet to know Me as I truly am.

Peace, treasured child. My justice and My mercy are not opposite qualities in My personality, contrary to many religious traditions. I AM not unjust to show mercy, nor am I unmerciful when I act with justice. The pious-sounding phrase, "God is not only merciful; He is just!" leaves the impression that I have opposite and conflicting natures. And that is a lie. I AM not double-minded.

Tenderhearted one, you must avoid the adamant railings of people entrapped in joyless religion. You must love them, but reject their errors, while allowing them to come to the end of themselves. Only when the self-righteous reach that place, will they find Me.

And when you hear the phrase "the fear of the Lord," bear in mind that there is more than one kind of fear. The true fear of the Lord has nothing to do with horror or dread. Ignorance of My true heart fosters that kind of terror, but My perfect love casts out all fear, for fear brings torment. In My way of thinking, "the fear of the Lord" is simply another way of saying, "the awe and gracious respect for the Lord." Do you suppose there could be a better way to think?

Yet the legalists are right about one thing; a great lack of "the fear of the Lord" plagues the church today. But surely the reason is obvious. How can people feel awe or gracious respect toward Someone they hardly know?

Yours sincerely,

Dad

# Day 52

First Corinthians 6:18-20;
Titus 2:11-14;
James 4:7-8

Pressured Child,

What do you do when lust nibbles at your emotions? Flee! Run for your life! I mean this. Lust withers and dies under the healing light of My love.

Draw near! Arise in the Anointing! Say no to temptation and watch it wither away. Better yet, say yes to My Spirit. The evil one seeks another platform when he loses the limelight of center stage.

Your invincible Refuge,

Dad

*Joshua 6; Proverbs 8:6-8;*
*Philippians 1:6*

Struggling One,

Why do you still doubt? Haven't I worked mighty miracles for you even recently? Of course this battle will not go on forever—certainly not for a lifetime! Do you really imagine that I would lead us to wage an unwinnable war? Have you ever known Me to give orders for their own sake? Or merely to please Myself? Don't you think if there existed anyone more qualified to take command I would let them?

Treasured child, you know that My throne is founded on love and wisdom, not brute force. I say a thing is right, not to make it right; I say a thing is right because it is right. Child, to obey My orders is not to grovel in subservience. It is to discover reality and to learn to reign with Me! When you follow My commands, you actually enact My tactics. You align with My design and thus find the path to freedom and peace.

If you recall, I once gave some very strange orders to Joshua and the fledgling Israeli nation. Who would ever have guessed that Jericho's walls would crumble at the sound of marching feet, trumpet blasts, and shouting voices? But they did, just the same. Knowing this, why do you grumble about "arbitrary mandates" from your Captain? You know quite well by now that I have always had a unique way of doing things. Carry on! We are in this together and we are too close to victory for quibbling questions! Besides, in the joy of our triumph you'll not remember them anyway.

Firmly, with fierce devotion,

Your Dad

# Day 54

Busy One,

Which do you prefer? Messy houses filled with laughter and love? Or tidy dwellings inhabited by uptight people?

In My view, the better homes and gardens are the user-friendly ones. I often link "neatness freaks" and "sloppy slouches" together to heal them. Don't you find My wisdom delightful?

Welcome back! I missed you.

Dad

*Hebrews 12:7-28*

Beloved Adventurer!

What is truth? Truth is timeless, everlasting fact. Truth is a word that describes the way reality is, was, and forever is bound to be. Two plus two equals four, blue mixed with yellow is green, and water will forever consist of two parts hydrogen and one part oxygen. There never was a time or a place where two plus two equaled nine, or blue and yellow made purple, or water was oil.

No, truth transcends the trends of human culture and opinion in the same way a real person transcends a cartoon character. Truth just is! And why? Because I AM! Solid, irreversible, universal Fact; I AM what I AM—and not even I can change that fact. There never was a time when I was called into existence, and neither is it possible that I should ever cease to exist. I cannot deny Myself, for I AM the Solid Rock. And you should be glad, questioning one.

When I tell you one path leads to life and another leads to death, do you not realize I AM merely showing you how reality happens to work? Child, I show you because I love you. I love you enough to care. Not only do I love you with My affections, I also love you with My ambitions, My aspirations. You might say I have a "champagne taste" where your interests are concerned. I do want the very best for you and, I will admit, My dreams for you are far higher than your young mind can even faintly grasp at the moment.

Honestly!

Dad

Beloved Truth-Seeker,

Are you asking for the gift of discerning of spirits or for the gift of fault-finding? Heavenly discernment detects at least two-thirds more angels than devils.

How can you pursue truth—uncompromising truth—and at the same time remain patient and loving? I'm glad you've asked! You must remember that the purpose of your pursuit is to enjoy deeper intimacy with Me—to find your own healing and freedom – and not to enforce a lifestyle upon others.

The mind of Christ is yours for the asking. Always!

Love,

Dad

My Courageous Conqueror,

Why not trust My ability to teach you even as I guide your steps? My Anointing rests upon you, and you need nothing else. Just commit your comings and goings to Me as you always have! The truths I AM teaching you now exceed the limits of words; otherwise I would have spoken them to you.

Yes, you are right. Lately I have been leading you into realms which, by their very nature, exclude the feasibility of receiving the counsel of men. Terribly wonderful of Me, is it not? I do know what I AM doing, child, though you have thought yourself unprepared for the recent changes. And I will say that some of your guesses as to their meaning have been...interesting.

Child, child! This is adventure, not adversity! Will you spoil it by complaining? Stop arguing and questioning! Rejoice! If you were unqualified I would not have brought you to this place. Trust Me, treasured one, I know what I AM doing—exactly.

Always!

Dad

Day 58

Matthew 5:9;
First Corinthians 13:4

Courageous Child,

My peacemakers act as blessed shock-absorbers in this world. They bear the brunt of the blows exchanged between the raging and the ruthless. Now you know how I feel. It hurts, doesn't it? Loving people who detest one another.

Thank you for putting up with the bull-headed, the pokey, the disorganized. Have you noticed My anointing? Expect rewards that will raise some envious eyebrows!

Yours proudly,

Dad

73

*Genesis 15:1-6, 21:1-7*

Truth Seeker,

Again, as I have said, nothing shall be impossible to him who believes! I AM making a way—a broad and level way in this present desert. Just as the Scriptures say, I truly am flooding the dry and empty places in your life with torrents of My living water, and I AM working the transformation you have long desired to see. How could I not? I AM the God of radical change!

But will you cooperate with Me in the process? Keep following Me, trusting My promises, just as your spiritual father Abraham did. As we both know, he was far from perfect, yet he did see the son of My promise brought to birth in a miraculous time and way. Yes, Isaac came kicking and squalling into this world despite the failures of his father. And why? Abraham practiced his faith—all the time.

When I called him from the land of his birth, he arose and left all that was familiar, altering his whole lifestyle to follow My call. He made his home in the land of My promise, though it meant living there as a stranger, an alien, and a nomad dwelling in tents for a season. What a stubborn man he was! He took Me at My word, acting like a founding father long before he ever was one. Lovable, indomitable Abraham—is it any wonder I AM not ashamed to be called his Father?

You see, that man willed to act upon My word even in those initial stages when his promised land seemed to promise nothing but a lunar landscape laughing at his dreams. Yet all who would know Me as the God of transformation—in principle—must reenact the acts of Abraham. Child, are you willing? The present desolation is but the preparation for your transformation; truly it is. You have chosen My land, and you will not be disappointed, I promise!

Abba

Little One,

Do you want bewilderment bombarding your mind for a lifetime? Then solicit everyone's opinion about everything. Teeter on a tightrope for people who couldn't care less and for those who are impossible to please. When I speak, refuse to respond until 10,000 confirmations arrive, hand-delivered by angels!

I assure you that opinionated personalities who never cease trying to alter others will find themselves isolated. Who can blame folks for dreading their company? How tragic that self-appointed purgers experience such loneliness! Yet, how fortunate are those who escape their tyranny.

Just listen to Me, child. Do not let the opinions of others imprison you.

Always your Friend, come what may, no matter what,

Abba

*First Corinthians 12:14-20*

Questioning Child,

I know your loved one has his irksome qualities, but he does have many strengths that you lack. I have brought you together to complete, not compete. Even those alternating feelings of irritation and compassion I have allowed for your strengthening. I will say it is wrong for you to keep second-guessing his motives and responses. Your brother is not as easy to read as you think but, warts and all, he is Mine (just as you are). He is, in fact, rather complex as mortals go, and even I find him complicated—in a delightful sort of way. But then again, you are not as simple as you imagine. So why not leave all the judging to Me? Let Me deal with him; do you mind?

My son does need your influence as much as you need his, but stop trying to influence him and relax. Just be joyful, considerate, and honest and, of course, be yourself. Also avoid all self-scrutiny not instigated by Me. And please! Stop apologizing for your every move. Why speak of problems no one else would ever think about unless you brought them to mind?

Relax! As I have already whispered to your heart, you both are being polished. Yes, you both are serving as sandpaper, each for the other (O glorious truth!); and, I humbly concede, the credit belongs to Me.

Count it all joy!

Dad

Dedicated Witness,

Which falls on your ears with greater credibility: "I love you," or "Yea verily, My soul languisheth after thee with bowels of tender mercies"?

Long faces, dark colors, somber voices intoning pious-sounding noises—do you find them impressive? Hidebound religiosity hides My heart from a hurting world. Thank you for being the down-to-earth blessing you truly are, child. You need never try to be anything or anyone else!

Abba

*First Corinthians 7:7*

Zealous Deliverer,

You cannot insist that others walk your walk or live out your calling. Surely you remember how long you were in reaching this place. I do. Understand, cherished one, I'm not scolding you, at all. No, every faltering step and every hesitation was worthwhile in view of your present development. But that is My point.

What now appears to you as mere reasonable service once loomed before your eyes as an impassable gulf, and many truths you would never think to question these days you once thought were utter nonsense. Ha! How well I remember!

Be patient, child. Just keep practicing what you know. Truth is its own advertisement—you know it is. Besides, your ability to succeed in your walk has nothing to do with other mortals walking it with you. You are not alone. I AM with you. Meanwhile, give your friends time to learn and room to grow as I have done for you. Not all learn the same lessons at the same time; but all do learn thoroughly. I see to that. After all, where do you think you got those stubborn tendencies of yours?

Dad

Bewildered Deliverer,

What is this "emptiness" you are feeling? I will tell you. You are in transition. In the midst of change there is no choice but to move. In the process of movement, settling in is out of the question. So of course you feel rootless! A tree being transplanted cannot be rooted until it is planted again in good soil.

Ponder this truth and remember it: there is no way to enjoy the comforts of a home and move at the same time. And it is impossible to harvest fruit from a vineyard yet to be.

I know it has seemed like a long journey, but it will be shorter if you will keep this in mind: you aren't supposed to feel satisfied where you are. This isn't home. This is travel.

Meantime, why not enjoy the scenery? You will never pass this way again, and one day you will cherish the memories of this trip, if you will take note of them now. Otherwise, you might arrive at point "B" with no stories to tell!

Helpfully,

Dad

Worried One,

It is nonsense to fear aging, because everyone will grow older. Has it occurred to you that every stage of life offers unique advantages and privileges?

I will not allow you to suffer abandonment in old age. Your sunset years promise a harvest of success, saturated with multiplied kindness and mercy. Hold to this promise! It is yours.

The Ancient of Days,

Your Dad

Day 66

Dear Child,

Again you have delighted My heart by your willingness to give. Forsake all fears of having given unwisely and commit the memories of your offerings to Me. No longer look back. Forsake questioning. I AM the One who has led you to give all you have given and I will bless your offerings. I will multiply all back to you again—soon. Very soon, in fact.

Meanwhile, avoid the pitfalls of haste and presumption and abide in My peace. Be steadfast. Decide to abide. Refuse all rationalization or any thought luring you into the frenzy of frantic grasping and self-reliance. Any action taken with even a hint of impatience or fear can never be an act of faith. No, faith is a solid knowledge of the heart, not a groping, grasping guess of the mind. Faith is far more than believing. Faith is knowing. It is a knowing arising from an inner reality seeded into your spirit by My Spirit. Yes, faith—true faith—is the unshakable conviction that those things you have desired have already been provided. And believe Me, cherished conqueror—they have!

Gladly,

Dad

Concerned Conqueror,

Those captivated by the occult thirst for My power. They've scrapped sterile religion to search for it elsewhere. And rightly so! Which is worse? The mad reign of hell-based religiosity or the magic of mesmerizers? They both appear identical to Me! Only mercy-miracles can woo wounded hearts away from such slavery.

Actually, I AM the Higher Power that they have been searching for, and the Best Friend they will ever have. If you long to know what I AM like, study Jesus. I AM delighted in the interest you are showing. Be prepared for miracles! I will make a believer out of you yet!

Yours supernaturally, naturally,

Abba

# Day 68

Lonely Liberator,

I know. Your grief has been a silent one, shared only by Me, but I will remind you again that in the solitude of secret sorrows, saviors are formed. Small comfort though it may now seem to be, will you walk on with Me in the knowledge of this? I have borne your griefs, carried your sorrows, and fully understood your stumblings. And I have not left you. No, not for a moment. And I AM with you now, holding you. I know how much you yearn to please Me, and the very strength of your desire touches My heart, as much as any gift you ever could give Me.

Knowing this, will you cease all striving and forsake all fear? Yes, child, put your mind at rest and reign with Me! Receive My forgiveness and reign from your position of peace. Offer the sacrifice of praise! And remember, I ask you to offer praise for your sake, not Mine. I AM entirely secure in Myself and need no reassurance of My worth or abilities. However, you actually need the transformed perspective that comes when you enter into praise. Your giving thanks in all things delights Me because it opens your eyes to see Me fulfilling My loving purpose in all things. This keeps you in constant contact with the healing energy of My Presence.

I want this for you. I want all your guilt feelings and grief to vanish. Most of all, I want you to see yourself as I see you. Do you yearn for the healing power of My Presence? Then enter into praise, child! It's time that you experience true and lasting peace, the peace that transcends human understanding.

Truly,

Dad

Fearful One,

If the son of an earthly father were to ask for bread, would he be given a stone? If he should ask for a fish, would he be given a serpent? You know the answer, so why do you allow those wicked caricatures of God portrayed by ignorant men to frighten you? Child, I appeal to your sense of common decency! Make a list of the qualities one would normally expect to find in a good earthly father! Contemplate fatherhood as it might be without human limitations or corruption, and you will begin to catch a glimpse of the real truth.

Do you honestly think I have some secret motive to disown you? To exploit you? To harass or humiliate you? Am I One to make promises and yet complicate them with hard conditions, rendering them irrelevant and void of fulfillment? Think, child! Think! For Heaven's sake, have a little trust, will you?

Imploringly,

Dad

Worried Worker,

Now that you are rigorously applying all of the rules, are you happy? Your treadmill existence seems a great bore to Me, but if it really satisfies you, I will not interfere—although I must admit, the goals you seek are quite different from Mine.

I know you find it hard to believe, but I often simply wish to converse and enjoy our friendship. I also have delightful gifts to share, but you are too busy.

Child, I only hope you are not doing all of that on My account—I certainly would never ask for it. Dead works are not My department. They are far too costly for you. If you ever get tired, will you please let Me know?

Tenderly concerned,

Dad

# Day 71

Wounded Soldier,

No, it is not your fault. I AM in control. Therefore, commit all "whys" and "wherefores" to Me. Unless you had finally reached the despair of achieving success by your own strength, how would you have come to learn My secrets? How else could you have learned that stubborn dependence upon Me, which is so obviously the key to the release of My power?

You need to keep in mind that Kingdom policy has always demanded that every upward flight first take on the appearance of a downward plunge. This the world has never understood.

I know. Conflicts have come and contradictions have come as well, but they have come to pass. They are but the labor pains preceding the birth of your new vision—our new vision.

What? Are you really worried about your reputation? Child, I AM not worried about Mine, so why should either of us be worried about yours? After all, your reputation is in very good hands—Mine.

Dad

ABBA CALLING

Little One,

Why do you question? Why now? If the promises I whispered to your heart were, as you have feared, merely the wishful thoughts of your mind, then why the fruit? Don't you see that even today you are in the midst of the fulfillment of My words? Rejoice! All promises are, at this very moment, in process. If you cannot believe My words, then will you believe Me for My works?

Review what I have already done! Allow Me to finish, child. Discipline your mind to patience. Practice patience, and be at peace. Think on other things. Be thankful. Enjoy!

Your Dad

# Day 73

Questioning Child,

Roots over-watered will rot. I allow dry seasons to spur your roots to reach deeper into the soil of My love. Thus rooted and grounded, you will stand impervious to life's storms.

Yes, I AM quiet much of the time, but you need quietness. And you need the life My Presence brings to you, moment by moment, far more than you need words.

Be at peace, and keep trusting! I AM answering your prayers. I love you too much to forsake you.

Abba

# Day 74

*Psalm 37:23-24;*
*John 14:27*

Cherished One,

You must become quiet and allow Me to lead you as I always have. I will not disappoint you; you will see. Now, will you turn your thoughts to Me and refuse to strive? You need not try to become anything, because what you already are is exactly what is needed where I AM leading you this day. Besides, if you will receive My peace and simply enjoy being yourself, you will put others at ease, and they will actually be seeing Me, and not you at all.

Be confident! Choose to assume My quiet and unruffled calm in every motion, transaction, and communication. Do you recall that Jesus promised, "My peace I give to you; My peace I leave with you"? So there you have it—peace is a gift you have already been given. Receive it. Draw strength from it. Walk in it. Be done with the stress of striving to impress.

Child, if you walk in stress your friends see Me less and the cycle of fear will continue. As you walk in My peace, My light will increase and My glory will cover and hide you. Then, those you have feared meeting face to face will not be able to see yours for seeing Mine.

Abba

Inquiring Restorer,

A near-suicide victim encased in splints and plaster doesn't need to hear rebuke for having violated natural law or morality. Sometimes a square meal helps more than a revelation. Love people!

Some are hurting too much to make heads or tails of theology. These hurting people need healing. Thank you for imparting hope to despairing hearts. So many accuse and point fingers! So few comfort and heal. Good work!

Yours joyfully,

Dad

# Day 76

Treasured Child,

Whether a thing brings pleasure has nothing to do with its being right or wrong! Though some balk at the idea, more often than not you can discover Me in the fun and enjoyable things of life. Are you surprised? Come now! Who ever drummed up the silly notion that I oppose pleasure? Nonsense. Who do you think began the dance of the constellations? Were not the worlds sung into being amidst angelic shouts of joy?

Of course, we both know many things do offer certain short-lived pleasures, but such joys are deceptive and cruel, for they promise happiness while they actually produce death. These—but only these—are the pleasures I would withhold from you, cherished one.

Now shall I tell you the way to real joy? I call it the way of surrender. It is a straight and narrow path, but it does lead to pleasure. Hearty, robust, pure pleasure.

Isn't this what you want? Then surrender your desires, each one of them, to Me! Yes, child. Yield every desire to My Spirit, and you will find you are filled with a joy eclipsing all else.

Then having surrendered to My Spirit, do as you wish! And you may as well be prepared—many surprises await you. The way I see it, your problem has been the lack of pleasure—real pleasure, that is.

So you think I'm stodgy, somber, old-fashioned? Ha! Follow Me, and you will see. I remain,

> Everlastingly young and the Ancient of Days,
> Your Dad

Waiting One,

Be patient. I will bring to pass all I have promised. What now seems to you a needless delay—even a backward move—is actually an important step in the necessary process. Child, the pains of healing are similar to the pains of the earlier difficulty, but with one significant difference: they are the result of the steady flow of My Life which is, even now, reversing the damages you have asked Me to mend.

Keep your eyes on Me, for I know an important principle you have forgotten. Often what is quickly acquired is also quickly lost. Therefore, rest! I AM laying a solid foundation that cannot be moved.

Faithfully,

Dad

Diligent Disciple,

Yes, it has been hard, I know, but that tough training period is nearly over now. As I told you before, I have made use of this challenging season to prepare you for promotion, not to punish you. I have been trusting you to trust Me. Thank you for trusting! I realize it has not been easy.

I especially want to thank you for listening for My voice when all those other conflicting voices arose. I know how hard it was—especially when all the others thought they were hearing from Me and kept telling you that you were not. But you were, child. Believe Me, you were! Because you wanted My will above all else, you found it after all.

Now do you see the fruit of those days? You have learned to hear My voice above all the clamor and you are stronger—more resilient. Anyone who really knows you can see it. How can I describe My joy? At last! You chose to stand fast. You set your heart to trust Me, even in those times when the enemy told you I had left you and you had missed the way.

And what about your tantrums? I never took them seriously. They certainly never offended Me. As is often the case with My children, the frustration expressed by your lips had nothing to do with the deeper faith of your heart, expressed by your will to follow Me. When you told Me you were trusting Me and then willed to walk on with Me, I took you at your word.

I admit, you did ask your fair share of hard questions. But consider My servant Job. He did the same, do you recall? My assessment is this: in all your railing and flailing you never sinned, though we both know your patience did wear thin at times. Dangerously thin. But after all, you were being stretched to your very limits, were you not? I think so.

Stop feeling guilty and enjoy your rest. The rest is a part of the training too. New joys, new powers, and new conquests await you, but I do want you to be prepared to enjoy them!

Delightedly,

Dad

Terse Child,

Pouting keeps everyone guessing, doesn't it? Furious work done in quiet rage with tight lips makes people tremble and walk softly! And you are demanding that I grant you more authority? Ha!

Right. Loving Me is one thing; putting up with people is another! Or so it seems to your jangled nerves at the moment. Will you pause and receive My refreshment?

With deepest understanding,

Dad

Weary One,

Ministry means servanthood. Being a servant means serving without being thanked or recognized. It often entails giving and going unnoticed, being tired and not rested, sorrowful and not comforted. Servanthood by its very nature implies working behind the scenes, and it always demands quiet reliability on the part of the servant.

Ministry does not mean business career. Neither does it mean hobby or pastime. The term "ministry" is light-years removed from the concept of theatrical performance or show business. Ministry can function in these fields, of course. And it should. But the heart of ministry is to serve, not to shine.

I realize you've been shuttled about lately, ignored and taken for granted. You have also wondered if those to whom you have ministered ever stopped to consider your own private life and needs. Does it matter? Why do you worry about them? Why do you seek their honor when you have Mine?

Sincerely!

Dad

*Proverbs 8:17*

Pressured Restorer,

Be encouraged and continue to wait quietly. I AM allowing this waiting season to show you the joy—and the power—of My calming Presence. Haven't I promised that if you seek Me with all of your heart you will find Me? A rich discovery awaits you, be assured. However, the syndrome of frantically seeking Me only in moments of adversity must end. You have not understood, My dear child, but most of the stress compelling you to call out to Me for solutions will end when you discover the joy of constant fellowship with Me.

And yes—I have heard your prayers, and you are right. I have not answered them yet. Why? Child, I have far more to give you than you have asked Me to give. I would not have you settle for less.

Patiently,

Dad

Treasured Restorer,

I repeat: Refuse to fear, for I AM with you. Do not despair, for I AM your God. I will strengthen and help you. I will uphold you with My righteous right hand. Even now I AM fulfilling these words!

Just to confirm—you are on the brink of a breakthrough! Not a breakdown, but a breakthrough. Birth pains often feel like death pangs, weary one. You needn't strive. I AM holding you, protecting you, guiding you.

Faithfully,

Abba

# Day 83

Fearless Freedom Fighter,

The vision will be fulfilled, but as I told you before, My priority is you, not your work. At present I AM rebuilding your walls, in a manner of speaking, but there is rubble that first must be swept away. Now I AM showing you what the rubble is, why it came to be, and how it is to be removed. So be patient with yourself, and be patient with Me.

Some of the rubble is bits and pieces of an earlier "you" that was truly good, but was destroyed when the enemy took advantage of your youth. Trust Me to finish the job of clearing it away. You are becoming a new and glorious temple! I AM making all things new, and the splendor of the new will far surpass the glory of the old. The sooner the old ruins are removed, the sooner the new "you" will emerge. Therefore, work in joy and in hope! I AM with you.

And what of those odd-shaped fragments? Surely you recall? Those are scraps from the materials you used when you once set out to rebuild your own walls! Do you remember your rage when I sent the rains to wreck that dreadful little project? I do. We can laugh about it together now, of course. Thankfully, the plan was aborted before it really began to take shape. And now, that will mean less work and time saved for both of us—provided you resist the urge to analyze every piece and get on with the job of clearing them out.

And do bear in mind that your walls will be altogether unlike your foundations. It would be wrong to expect the same materials and procedures at this point. Walls are not supposed to be made like foundations; they are supposed to be made like walls. Remember this. Enjoy the new! Keep working in hope! I AM!

Abba

*Ephesians 1:7-8; 6:17-18*

Searching Child,

How do I speak? Through all that Jesus is, represents, and declares. Also, through Scripture. Through impressions. Through situations. Through experience, through nature, through people. Sometimes hands and feet hear Me better than heads do!

I know. You long to help people, not hurt them. Learn to trust My still small voice, and enjoy awe-inspiring protection and wisdom. I've noted your sacrifices. Enjoy living!

I AM supporting you,

Dad

Happy Adventurer,

Sanctimony prefers procedure to people. True sanctity prefers people to procedure. Yes, the Sabbath is for man, not man for the Sabbath, and if you follow this rule you will find your heart always aligned with Mine.

The sanctimonious work for the applause of people, but the sanctified work to bless and help people. Shallow religiosity seeks the limelight. Authentic spirituality seeks Heaven's light—for everyone.

Now will you let this dispel those worries of yours about sanctification? Personally, I think you would be happier with more of it. Furthermore, I think you agree!

Honestly, but cheerfully,

Dad

Romans 8:26;
First Corinthians 1:4-9;
2:9-13; 13:8-12

Thirsting Truth Seeker,

I've prepared riches for you that transcend mortal imagination. My Spirit will cause you to realize, know, and experience them.

Do you realize that My Spirit actually prays inside you? Yes, He is leading you beyond the limits of mere words along the path of My wisdom and provision. Who said that miracles ceased after the death of the last apostle? I didn't! Don't cheat yourself. Expect supernatural surprises!

Yours with delight,

Dad

# Day 87

Daring Deliverer,

Why are you so depressed? Why do you think the enemy sends his unwitting pawns to discourage you? His ploy is to unravel your resolve and courage!

I never commissioned you to argue, persuade, or answer all questions. You know very well that My wisdom reveals itself in power, not in talk. Anyone can talk! Do you recall that I once empowered a fine donkey of Mine to demonstrate this to a foolish prophet? Obviously, that noble beast had more prophetic insight than did her master—agreed?

Resettle yourself in My calm, unruffled serenity. Enjoy living again! I called you to demonstrate My power—to free people, not to please them. So resume doing what I have anointed you to do! In this world there is no painless way to love; I know. But carry on. Forgive the faultfinders, forget your doubts, and just be the blessing you are. To dance to the tune of your critics only delays their deliverance and turns your joy into drudgery.

Rejoice! I AM trusting you! Take up the Shield of Faith again, child. Join with Me in advancing our Kingdom of Light in this despair-darkened world. Resume listening to the gentle voice of My Spirit and behold My power in action. I AM with you. We are in this mission together. And remember! My success does not depend on yours; yours depends on Mine! Yes, I realize this flatly contradicts religious views widely advertised these days. As you well know, I love smashing sacred cows!

Yours with delight,
Dad

P.S. You weren't making up the script as you blundered your way through. A prophetic lifestyle just feels that way. Good work!

Pressured Child,

Constructive criticism can feel very draining to people who are already exhausted and spent, so instead of sharing your helpful insights today, why not shower encouragement? Pure encouragement, undiluted with tactful reservations or timely hints. Look for the praiseworthy things and celebrate them! Applaud them! Praise your loved ones and fellow workers! Your encouragement will strengthen them to excel far beyond the levels of performance that any critical analysis might bring.

This is My way with you. Aren't you glad?

Loving you always,

Dad

Devoted Worshiper,

Your songs of praise—how can I describe the joy they release in My Spirit? Worship is not simply an act of the will. Worship arises as a natural response when human hearts awaken to the wonder of My Abiding Presence, My Limitless Love; and it is My job to bring you into this realization, not yours.

Peace, tender one. I AM with you! Be still, and know that I AM God. You make moving mountains sheer pleasure today.

Your almighty Refuge,

Dad

Bold Pioneer,

I repeat—you must keep your focus on My faithfulness, not on how things appear to your natural eyes. Then you can remain calm in the face of sudden obstacles and even satanic harassments. Jesus experienced these things and so will you. But you can retain your serenity and sanity by remembering that I AM with you.

Why do I let you seem to make messes at times, despite all your precautions and prayers? For one thing, I AM keeping you flexible. I'm also taking yet another opportunity to show you how I AM causing all things—your blunders included—to work together for our mutual joy and blessing.

Now, let's talk about a spiritual principle at work called buffeting. Believe Me, treasured one, all who experience My Spirit's leading will encounter this principle, sooner or later. Even the apostle Paul blundered into obstacles and meaningless opposition. For long seasons he wondered why his prayers seemed to bounce back to him unanswered. And, like yourself, he felt the pain of people criticizing instead of helping him as he labored in weakness and exhaustion.

Why do I allow buffeting? Dear child, too much easy success would make you unbearable. Honestly! So I let the buffeting come to help you mature and acquire increased endurance. I also use those small flaws of yours to help you form the habit of casting yourself into My arms. This habit will cause you to reflect My likeness—My glory—with increasing clarity and splendor. And while this is happening, your remaining imperfections beam a ray of hope to others who, like yourself, need constant reassurance that I love and work through imperfect people.

Yours with deepest devotion,
Abba

# Day 91

*Proverbs 16:32;*
*Lamentations 3:31-33;*
*Ephesians 4:26-27*

Seething Servant,

Sorry that everything and everyone annoys you right now. It's an interesting challenge for Omnipresence—but I'm doing My best to stay out of your way! Of course, when you need Me, I AM always available.

I can become annoyed, true enough. But I remain mad for only a moment. I AM shaping you to become as I AM. Aren't you glad? No doubt you've noticed that those who seethe with rage around the clock suffer burnout!

Protecting you always,

Dad

Chosen Deliverer,

I AM the One who called you, so will you believe Me? I believe in you, and that is all that matters. Too late? How could that be, cherished one? It is never too late when you are in My care, for all times are Mine, yours included.

Trust Me! Even if you had missed the mark ten thousand times ten thousand, I still make all things new. Your every step, however faltering, and your every setback, I will use to the utmost good in My economy. You will see! I have designed and destined you to be a compassionate deliverer, and you will have healing gifts to share. As you share them, you will spare many the heartaches you have known.

Already I AM multiplying the good you accomplished during your wayward years of wandering. I AM delighted to reckon all as done unto Me, so I AM accounting your every act of love to the record of your faithful service.

Now accept My gifts and cease sputtering all that nonsense about your unworthiness. Am I unable to determine just wages for My workers? Subject closed. Enough! Let Me dry those tears. You will need clear vision to enter the new door I AM now opening for you.

And never fret about having too little time left. Bear in mind that I am famous for doing remarkable things with very small quantities. Do you recall how Christ fed the multitudes with a mere five loaves of bread and two fish? Actually, that miracle of multiplication was one of My more modest ones.

I have much more to tell you, and I will, as you learn and grow. But there is no reason to rush, child. We have Eternity ahead of us. I AM the King of all Ages. I AM the Master of all times—including yours. Time without end—I AM!

Yours forever,

Dad

Cherished Restorer,

What is the "local church"? It is My royal children loving their neighbors.

I love you just as you are. That explains why you're seeing healing emerge in your thoughts and behavior. All I ask is that you love others as I love you. And I love you too much to spare you from growing pains.

Ever trusting you,

Dad

Cherished One,

Self-control is not willpower. Have you noticed? Self-control truly is a fruit of the Spirit. It is a result. It is a by-product of Spirit-inspired vision. Self-control derives its strength from the passion of knowing your purpose and pursuing it. When you know that, when a clear picture of your royal destiny captivates your heart, nothing—good or bad—can distract you.

I want you to see your purpose. I want to flood your spirit with a vision of your mission—daily. When you see Whose you are, what you are, and what you are about, you will easily avoid those things you can do without.

I treasure your friendship and long to show you how to order your days and maximize your joy. So thanks for taking time for us. Remember, the vision that I give you empowers you to be the blessing to the world that you long to be. And that vision is My gift to you, always. Don't forget! Omnipotence supports you!

Always,

Abba

Discouraged Child,

Yes, you live in a harsh world. It's a world that exhibits little patience with inexperience, lack of knowledge, or ineptitude.

Quickly enter into My rest, cherished one, and trust the gentle promptings of My Spirit within you. Learn to resist rushing, last-minute scrambling, stampeding! Steady plodding saves a soul from many a snare.

View sudden rearrangements as rescues. Fresh wisdom is coming, along with favor in the workplace.

Yours joyfully,

Dad

Frustrated Fighter,

Why have I been leading you through this obstacle course of pressured events? Why the unreasonable demands, the dangers? I have allowed them for one practical reason: to deliver you from fear once and for all.

I have known what you had yet to discover, child. Every exposure to the unexpected, the unreasonable, and the undeserved has been an inoculation of sorts. Oh yes, I do have all kinds of strategies—have you noticed? Yet have you noticed this? More and more you are coming to trust Me; less and less you are fearing the future. You see, every time those threats have reared their silly heads, I have repeatedly shown you My power to bring them to naught. And I have been building an inner peace in you at the same time.

Do you realize how much more pleasant your company has become lately? Ah yes, the new you is far easier to enjoy—I assure you. Everyone is glad about that. But, no doubt, you are the most glad of all!

Proudly, joyfully,

Dad

Intense Trooper,

I really do want you to enjoy your life. Take time to laugh, sing, dance, and spread mirth. Take time for your friends and loved ones. Take time for frolic with children and even animals. I do! For Heaven's sake, lighten up! Will you?

Hard-liners nearly always rear children who become compromisers—or rebels. The offspring of compromisers and rebels often lash out to become hard-liners. Hearing My voice heals all.

Yours joyfully,

Dad

Treasured Child,

Your servant's heart delights Me, but do you mind if I ask a few personal questions? Why do you weary yourself rushing about looking for things to do, leaving Me behind to watch? Is it really Kingdom business you are doing? Or are you trying to earn My love?

But child! How can you earn what you already have? Are you seeking to earn the love of mere mortals? If their love can be bought, it is false. Why do you toil for that which is not Bread and settle for worthless wages?

Come home. Trust Me to take care of the details that obsess you. Let Me refresh you. My heart aches for your weariness and pain.

Tenderly,

Abba

Dedicated Disciple,

Do you realize the command to "fret not" carries equal weight with any other command of Mine? Think about it.

What do you suppose would become of the more obvious sins of covetousness, revenge, and infidelity if worry were forever banished? Worry is but another form of fear—agreed?

Worry is always wrong. It amounts to doubting My ability to protect and provide for you. It is lethal to the heart.

In everything give thanks, child! And your thanks will establish what your mind thinks. Always.

By the way, have you ever paused to ponder how often I think about you? I think you'd be amazed if you knew.

Love,

Dad

*Romans 8:28*

Questioning One,

Why do you worry about "wasted" time? Child, you have experienced some errors and a few false starts, but never mind. Redeeming time and fresh beginnings are two of My mightiest mercies! Follow Me! I will cause every reversal to count as rehearsal for even greater victories than were previously planned.

Child, I make all things new, including you. Will you rest in this assurance? I AM the Master of time, and there is no loss in Me.

Truly!

Abba

# Day 101

Sorrowful One,

If you were trying to live two lifestyles, if you were justifying sin or seeking to harm another, that would be different. Then I would be forced to let you feel the full impact of your ways. I would laugh at your reasonings, ignore your pretended prayers, and weep for your delusion. But such is not the case. I told you this earlier, but I will tell you again: I have seen your tears and heard your cries. I AM holding you now.

Don't give up. I haven't. Your sacrifices of praise and even your outbursts of frustration are all part of a two-fold process. You are experiencing the death throes of the old and the birth pains of the new, and there just is no other way for this deliverance to come forth. Soon you'll not even think to question the process. You'll be too busy enjoying the substance born of the process.

Remember, I cannot lie.

Faithfully,

Your Dad

Loving Liberator,

Sometimes My mercy arrives as judgment. Could I be merciful and let evil reign unrestrained in your world? Just allow Me to do the judging. This burden is too heavy for you.

To understand the Bible, you must view it in the pure light of My unfailing love. Mercy triumphs over judgment. Always! In other words, mercy motivates my judgment. That is the Bible's message—bottom line. I love you. Go back and take another look.

Tenderly,

Dad

*Isaiah 52:14;*
*John 3:16*

Worried Child,

I AM just, pure, and holy. My love is limitless and seeks not its own. When those dark thoughts cloud your mind, causing you to question My love, I ask that you do one thing: remember the cross.

See it now. See the One crucified. See the humiliation, the horror of Innocence disrobed, mutilated, and bleeding. Pain racks His every atom. Each gasp of air is agony untold. His every nerve is a conduit of fire.

Can you hear Him cry? No one else can either, but I can. I hear it forever. How could I forget it? It's almost the sound of a boy—a stifled, intermittent cry it is.

No, child, don't turn away. Not yet, please. Do you see the thorns piercing His brow? The disfigurement of His face? The spikes splitting His hands and His feet? The jeering crowds at the foot of His cross? They didn't kill Him. They would have if they could have—but they could not. He gave His life. He shielded His enemies who were worthy of death by dying Himself in their stead. He suffered murder to save His murderers. He suffered shame to save His mockers.

And He would do it again. Again and again. And so would I. Is this not the destiny of Perfect Love in a fallen world?

This is the way love is, and this is the way I AM. Never forget it.

Entreatingly,

Abba

Beloved Conqueror,

I spoke, and the universe sprang into existence! I merely breathed, and swirling galaxies burst into being and constellations appeared, dancing in solemn procession. And you worry about money or the oppression of people? Ha!

Expect supply to arrive soon! When the money rolls in, will you still have time for our friendship? A penny for your thoughts.

Yours affectionately,

Dad

Recovering Restorer,

Be at peace. Know you are protected. Yes, you are right. I have allowed a lonely path for you—a path others have assessed from their surface view as an easy one. Never mind. You and I know differently and it is our view that counts, not theirs.

Rejoice! You are specially chosen and hand-picked. I have called you to reveal My heart to a hurting generation. The world is weary of words and so am I. Therefore I AM raising up an army of saviors, and as a leader in that army you have been chosen to demonstrate My saving character to many silent sufferers. For so long I have yearned, through My family, to love into wholeness the broken and wounded. You will exemplify how it is done.

Be at peace about your lack of knowledge. I have purposely foiled your attempts to become a theological expert. I need redeemers, not religionists. And why have I allowed you to work in weakness? To carry a burden that has forced you to fall continually upon My grace? I seek deliverers, not destroyers. Restorers, not rejecters. Your own need of mercy has made you an amazing fountain of mercy—a compassionate counselor and life-giver. You know it is true. I have kept you, formed you, withstood you at times, but always upheld you. And I have counted it all pure joy!

So you thought you would never be free, did you? Now do you see the purpose of those years of searching? Your seeming lack of solutions? These laid the foundation for your freedom today. Keep giving grace and keep loving sinners. I do. And stay committed to the good news of My power.

I AM!
Abba

Dear Child,

When you are seeking Me and surrendering your steps to My strategies, when you are pursuing truth with all your heart, forget the flak. Cease worrying about your lack and stop hesitating about decisions. Make choices! Trust Me with the results and refuse to judge the fruit of your work until I clearly lead you to do so.

All things are not as they at first appear to be. Start seeing all interruptions and confrontations, shortages and surprises, not as obstacles, but opportunities. These give you cause to pause—to rest—while I resolve. Your resting will release you into revelation otherwise unobtainable.

And remember. Today is one of those tomorrows you asked Me to keep many yesterdays ago. I AM.

Always,

Your Abba

Concerned Conqueror,

Not all in authority are out to get the little guy. Not all of them lust for position or power. Ordinarily, today's bosses are yesteryear's flunkies (frightened, like yourself) scrambling to do a job nobody appreciates or wants! Can you relate? Spectators find it easy to criticize.

Your fellow workers don't expect perfection from you. You'll be amazed by how just showing basic reliability will impress them! It takes time to establish a track record. Keep up the good work!

All powerfully yours,

Abba

Questioning Conqueror,

How many times must I tell you? This is warfare, not a pleasure cruise. True, I did promise that if you asked for a good gift I would not give you a counterfeit. But I never promised easy solutions and quick fixes. I did promise you Myself, but you have yet to appreciate the magnitude of that promise.

You do seem to have a problem with waiting, don't you? Has it occurred to you that your impatience may just be the problem? Child, I AM not scolding you, nor do your questions offend Me. I just want you to realize that this is not a mere skirmish; we have set out to win a war. So a few delays and setbacks are business as usual. They shouldn't devour your hope.

Would a well-seasoned soldier consider a battering ram useless, simply because it fails to smash the enemy's stronghold in a single thrust? Of course not. Your prayers—those times you spend walking and talking with Me in solitude—are exactly like a battering ram. In fact, our communication, in itself, is the most powerful weapon you possess. So use it!

By the way, if you're waiting to become "worthy," please stop. Long before time or worlds, Christ made you worthy. That is the Gospel truth. Walk in it.

Love,

Dad

# Day 109

Psalm 34:8; 46:10;
First Corinthians 4:20

Tired Disciple,

Overloaded with opinions? Befuddled by too many words and formulas bombarding your mind? Tired of hearing teaching, teaching, and more teaching?

Good! At last you're realizing that nothing can replace the sheer joy of My Presence, of experiencing My Essence! Constant drilling into "deep issues" makes for a boring mind. Can't we just hug sometimes?

Remember the rubbing-off effect of My Presence.

Yours joyfully, always,

Dad

Day 110

Worried Warrior,

Always remember. I AM Love, and Love never fails. Love cannot fail. Repeat this truth again and again. Commit it to memory. Let it saturate the deepest recesses of your being. And never forget! All that the Bible teaches about Love, including loving your neighbor as yourself, applies first to Me.

Love thinks evil of no one. It is not rude nor overbearing, but kind. Love is not proud nor easily offended. It never holds grudges. Love redeems and never rejects. Further, Love looks for the praiseworthy, always, and it does not seek its own interests.

You must learn to think of Me in this way, for this is the way I AM. Why believe the corrupted conceptions of legalistic religion? Hasn't your own experience confirmed the truth? Believe in the God who has saved you, many times. If I were looking for reasons to reject you, I could not be Who and What I AM—limitless, Holy Love.

Contrary to various religious traditions, love and holiness are not opposite qualities in My nature. I AM not two-faced nor am I double-minded. Therefore, any message of "holiness" that fosters hopelessness is of hell, not Heaven. Remember this. Any use of Scripture that spawns despair is warped and sinful. Many can parrot the Scriptures, but who can impart My love? I AM counting on you.

Peace. Your sins are forgiven.

Truly,

Abba

# Day III

Luke 1:50-53;
18:10-14;
James 2:12-13

Defensive One,

When you stop justifying yourself, I will justify you. I long to grant you miraculous mercy! But I can show mercy only to those who realize they need it. I love you. That is why I tell you the truth.

Mercy triumphs over judgment! This means love throws a party when people don't have to pay through the nose for their blunders. What inspires you to celebrate? Just asking.

Yours with deepest understanding,

Dad

ABBA CALLING

Searching Child,

How many times do you think Jesus taught about going the second mile or forgiving one's enemies or seeking first the Kingdom? He repeated Himself constantly, as any good teacher should. So it is a mistake to adopt the mentality that your every word must fall on the ears of your hearers as something "new."

My Son came to impart life, not to titillate fickle minds with original-sounding novelties. All that He did, said, or thought, and all that He *was,* transmitted life-giving grace and truth. He wasted no efforts trying to be "fresh" or "stimulating." But He did spend time with Me.

And what your Lord learned in My fellowship affected Him so profoundly that the power of My Presence permeated His life in every aspect. As a result, though He never tried to be interesting, He was. Your Lord was sometimes accused of having a demon, but no one ever called Him boring. Christ never sought originality, but throughout history His friends and His enemies alike have declared Him to be the Original among originals. He never studied a course in psychology, nor did He seek the advice of the "image consultants" of the day. Yet there never lived a man more powerful, more persuasive, or more convincing than Jesus of Nazareth. That is why the authorities had Him crucified. They feared the Nazarene might change the face of history. And He did. All by walking with Me.

Helpfully,

Dad

*Matthew 23:13-15;*
*John 14:26-27*

Disillusioned One,

One could say that I AM addicted to authenticity—hopelessly so. The best way to escape sharing My addiction is to avoid My company. But that amounts to a full-time career, doesn't it?

Never fear. Legalistic religion exists to furnish the public with the job skills to succeed! How I rejoice that, at last, you're seeing through that silly hocus-pocus.

I love you too much to let you live in illusion.

Truly!

Dad

# Day 114

Compassionate Deliverer,

A desert experience nearly always follows a time of fresh spiritual empowerment. Your Lord experienced this when His ministry began. My Spirit descended upon Him like a dove and, amazing as it seems, immediately drove Him into a wilderness of fasting and temptation.

His life is the master plan for all My anointed deliverers. Jesus truly is the Way, the Truth, and the Life. As the Dove led Him into My purposes and the desert prepared Him for power, so it will be for you and for all who aspire to do the mighty works of Jesus. That pattern can never change. Those who would be My healing agents in a suffering world must endure testing, for the passage of My power demands the durability that only the tests can build.

Now do you understand the aching void you so often feel after your mightiest victories? The vulnerability? The sheer terror of falling? My Spirit, by virtue of the pure Life He is, floods to the surface your flaws. And this is for your sake. By that He spares you the ruin that would result from the co-habitation of His fire with your flesh. His purpose is to purify, not to harm you—to prepare you for even greater capacity to transmit My power.

Let this truth keep you joyful, treasured one. Be tempered by the testings that follow the anointing, and you will wear the crown of life. Even more, you will wield the authority of that crown and do the powerful works of Jesus! I promise.

Abba

Treasured Child,

Has it occurred to your mind that I don't know how to forget you? A mad world may lock you up and throw away the key, but I hold in My possession a Key that opens all doors!

Never forget it. I have not forgotten you for a moment. Trust My timing. I love you too much to forget you.

Tenderly,

Abba

Pressured Peacemaker,

Let Me vindicate you. Trust Me to be the all-powerful Father that you proclaim and know Me to be. Stop worrying about your brother's opinion and go on doing what I have called you to do.

You have sought to gain the understanding of one who has much to learn before any of your words can even begin to make sense to his mind. You have tried to win his heart. Well done. You have tried—earnestly tried—and I have seen it and I AM pleased. Now will you leave the results to Me? You will like what I accomplish, I assure you!

Cease all self-castigations, all self-justifications, and all your rationalizations now. Henceforth I will do the correcting, the defending, the explaining. And you? You will be happy again. And I do think it's time you were.

Truly!

Dad

# Day 117

Habakkuk 2:18-19;
Galatians 5:25;
First John 5:21

Grieving Child,

My heart aches for your sorrow. I didn't laugh when your idol fell from its pedestal. I regret the grief idolatry has caused you. Consider it a violent rescue.

Idolatry betrays its presence through inflexibility. Worshiping inanimate gods turns hearts into stone or metal. It doesn't anger Me that you resist change, little one. All I AM asking is why do you fear it? Think about it.

I love you too much to let idolatry destroy you. Keep it simple! It is possible. Just follow Me.

With liberating love,

Abba

Questioning Conqueror,

You exercise more influence than you realize, and your insights carry more weight than you know. Your low assessment of your value is quite different from the admirable impression you leave with others, so stop listening to lies. Start trusting your gifts and stop trusting those doubts! If the enemy can persuade you to abdicate, not only will he score a victory against you, but he also will rob others. He will deny them the benefits you alone were designed to deliver.

I know. You feel inept, insecure, and insignificant. At times you feel as inexperienced as a child. But strange as it seems, I AM healing you of this mindset by promoting you. I AM now placing you in a position that demands more than you think you have to give.

Yes, at the moment you are being stretched. I want you to realize the prized possession you actually are to Me! I AM awakening potentials and unveiling gifts within you that you have been too blind to see. I AM purposely giving you some challenging assignments to break the confinements your heart has longed to escape. I want to rid you, once and for all, of that mediocre view you have held of yourself.

I understand your frustration. But as a sensible Father, I harbor no illusion that My children will always agree with My policies—at least, not at the outset. Nevertheless, I do expect them to trust the decisions of One who is older and wiser. Child, are you willing?

You will come to enjoy your new post, but you'll not have time to fret about that imagined inferiority of yours in the meanwhile. No, you'll be too busy, but I think you'll also be much happier. So for now I AM putting you in a strategic position to instruct others. I happen to know there is no better way for one to learn than to have to teach.

Cheer up! You are My creation, so isn't it reasonable to think that I must surely know more about you than you do?

Truly,

Dad

# Day 119

Searcher,

What is so wonderful about Jesus? In Him you discover Me, not only as I would appear and function in human form, but as your Friend who constantly lays down His life for you. No lesser god will ever satisfy you.

Jesus is the Way, the Truth, and the Life. Why? I cannot translate to human beings what I AM all about without Jesus! Ordinary people would find it impossible to relate to a God who never got bumps and bruises.

Truly,

Dad

# Day 120

Child of My Joy,

Why do you crave popularity with people when you're popular with Me? Nobody even begins to admire you as much as I do.

Everlasting arms enfold you. Love indestructible surrounds you. Power unlimited awaits your bidding. Hell shudders! We smile.

I will never change My mind about you. I think you're wonderful! Too wonderful to leave alone. Sorry you find this irksome at times.

I like you. There, I said it again.

Forever,

Dad

Beloved Rebel,

Believe it or not, I, too, find sterile religion boring—extremely boring. In fact, I often find it annoying. Has it occurred to you that I might be interested in many other subjects? I AM. My range of interest just might be even wider than yours!

I like various sports, arts, writing, music—and jokes. And although some would be shocked to hear it, I enjoy theater and dancing immensely. And why not? I AM the Inventor, if you recall. I also happen to be quite fond of animals. Or haven't you noticed? Oh yes, I AM an incurable bird watcher, and sparrows are some of My favorites. As you can see by looking around you, geography and astronomy never cease to captivate My interest. And you are living proof that I also delight in chemistry and microbiology.

However, you need to understand that mindless rituals, routines, and rigid rules are just as meaningless to Me as they are to you. I find much of the realm of organized religion to be very dull and drab. Its goals and interests are mostly unrelated to Mine. Many religious events I attend strictly from a sense of duty; you can be sure of that. I make it a policy to attend only if I AM invited, so, as you can surmise, I rarely go at all. By that I mean My heart is not in it. In one sense it would be impossible for Me not to be there. Perhaps that is what you might call one of the less fortunate aspects of being omnipresent?

We have more in common than you think! I find flowery speeches pointless, hide-bound tradition abusive, and I detest pompous religiosity. But I do love people. That is why I can't just simply give up on the Church. But isn't that the way love is? Love doesn't have an "off and on" switch. At least, My kind never has.

Besides, when I think of the Church I don't think of steeples and spires. I think of My compassionate family of liberators I have called to heal a wounded world. In My view, the religious rat race is a universe removed from what the Church is really about.

Keep an open mind and an open heart. I AM arranging some new contacts I think you're going to like.

All My Love,

Dad

ABBA CALLING

Determined Deliverer,

You will never do what? Say it again. I like challenges!

I AM not asking you to change your habits, child. I only ask that you bask in My love. Sounds somehow too simple, doesn't it? Your world underestimates the might of Omnipotent Love.

Just another warning. Never say "never" unless you're dying to do it.

Yours chuckling,

Abba

# Day 123.

Hurting Child,

Forgiveness is not a feeling; it is a choice. I AM with you, holding you close to My heart, and with My help, you can choose to forgive. Never fear, the feeling will follow. You will see.

I understand. The memories of the rejections, the betrayals and deceptions do have a way of seeping back to the surface of your mind. But have you ever stopped to think about why? They always return when you withdraw into negative analysis and neglect to enjoy the gifts I have showered upon you.

Of course, as you have noticed, I do keep sending distractions and interruptions to draw you away from unhealthy introspection. I also divert your plans to guard you from those who talk too much about the past. I shield you continually, but I cannot protect you from you. You have asked that I heal your broken heart, but will you cooperate with Me? Stop analyzing yourself and others, please. Allow Me to suture the wound.

I want you to get on with enjoying your life! New delights await you, and I want you to experience them. But how will you ever see what lies ahead if you keep looking behind? Forgive and forget, child. I do—constantly. But surely you have noticed by now? I do it gladly, with no regrets, all the time.

Tenderly yours,

Dad

Pressured Conqueror,

What happened to all your joy? Beware of joy-killers, popping in out of nowhere and annihilating liberty in "Jesus' name." Such ministries only spread misery in a world already despairing of hope.

Do you hear the music? At this moment I AM singing for joy over you. Thank you for caring about people.

Loving you always,

Dad

*Ephesians 4:26-32*

Worried Child,

When I said I couldn't protect you from yourself, I didn't mean it in the way you understood it. Of course I protect you from yourself! I do it all the time. I do it by softening the impact of the blows you inflict upon yourself when you act in haste, anger, or fear. But I cannot keep you from wielding those blows unless I destroy your power to choose.

Is that what you want? What sort of vegetable do you want to become? A plant with a human shape would be a remarkable curiosity in our Kingdom. Indeed it would. But the Image of My Son deserves a higher expression. At least, I think it does. Turning conquerors into cabbages is just not My department. That is the work of the enemy.

How does he do it? By deception, of course! He has no other power. When he teaches a man to habitually reject responsibility for his own actions and to see himself as a victim of fate, that man loses his grip on life. And the more entrenched in blame-placing and excuse-making he becomes, the more like a vegetable he becomes.

So don't you think it's time you stopped blaming others for your miseries? Take responsibility! Are you afraid to say "I'm sorry" or "I was wrong"? Don't be. It's not as bad as you think. Have you let the sins of others sour your outlook? Repent. You'll like the way it feels, I promise. Your happiness can be the responsibility of no one but yourself. No slight or wrong committed by anyone else can sabotage your joy, unless you let it. So forgive and forget. And as you do, also forgive yourself. I already have.

Forever with Love,
Dad

Bewildered Searcher,

Beware of the spirit of antichrist. He's always offering 666 easy steps to success without Jesus! His greatest lie is that the Lord of Glory cannot succeed, unless you do. What nonsense!

Thanks for listening and sparing yourself much exhaustion. Berserk as it appears, you are on the right path. You should see the ones I spared you from walking!

Lots of love, always,

Dad

Remorseful Restorer,

I foresaw your lapses. Looking back, you wonder why they happened at all. Because many of your mistakes appear so meaningless, when you view them from hindsight you often flush with shame. But may I tell you a secret?

I created you for success, but because I created you with freedom to choose, I knew that you sometimes would stumble. Knowing this, I planned in advance to permeate each day of your life with My mercies. Thus, all things—including your failures—must work together for your good while you are learning to live by My law of love. Remember, learning is a process. No one learns to walk without stumbling.

Lately you have been discovering how your lapses can become lessons to remind you of your need for My grace. Sustained "success" rooted in the strength of the flesh is superficial and deceptive. It is a glistening bubble that only the pin of an obvious sin can burst. No, I did not cause it, but I did allow it.

Understand. I want to save you from every sin, of course. But I don't want you just doing "right things." I want you doing right things for right reasons. I want you to be right inside. Why are you in such a hurry? I AM not. Frankly, those scrubby little uglies that have surfaced lately needed to become visible. You needed to see your inability. You also needed to see My love in action far more than you needed to see any outward show of success. Keep trusting My grace for your holiness. I AM!

Forever,

Your Dad

Child,

You are exactly where you need to be right now. Believe Me. If all external factors instantly changed, the lessons you are learning now would still be the same. The classroom could be a hotter one or a colder one, but it could not be a better one than this present one. There are many possible environments in which you could learn the truths I AM teaching you today. If you flee the present one, you will find another one, but I must warn you: it will be a harder one.

You asked Me to guide your steps, keep your tomorrows, and turn your blunders into blessings. Do you remember? Well, I have. I AM doing it right now, in fact.

Abba

Lovable Liberator,

You are angry, confused, and frustrated. This creates the depression. I allow the surprises to surface, not to confound you with sudden judgments or to harass you, but to train you. Have you heard of "rolling with the punches"? Or "bouncing back"? Or "taking things in stride"? These are the habits I AM teaching you now.

I want you to be resilient. I want you to be filled with tough faith. And I want you to be able to laugh at yourself while still liking yourself. Faith is not idealism. Faith is realism rooted in a settled joy that all things work together for your good.

Today's training is ingraining this conviction. Rejoice and be glad in it! I AM.

Everlastingly,

Your Dad

My Child,

A surrendered heart—a heart totally dependent upon My grace—is the greatest gift you can offer Me. I realize your difficulty. You fear the judgment of others. The idea of letting go—of turning loose of your struggles and abandoning your strategies—fills you with panic. "What if *they* see my lack, my emptiness?" you ask. "What will happen to my testimony, my witness?" I know all your fears.

Child, think! Who has promoted you and protected you thus far? Who has covered you, blessed you, given you favor, and empowered you? Do you honestly believe I would allow you to be brought to shame? Your own righteousness, your own works pose a greater threat to your public image than your trusting My grace ever has or ever will. But I have covered even these, have I not? Trust Me! Surrender all. Give Me room to act! What have you got to lose? Nothing but your vanity. Thankfully!

Forever in joy,

Your Dad

Frenzied Fighter,

My ways are not your ways. Again, I'm showing you a path you would have shunned, given the opportunity. And why? I lead you along the road of love—of giving. This road is not a thoroughfare, nor is it a way generally known even among seasoned travelers.

Today I want you to see purpose as I see it. Significance doesn't come from being seen. In our Kingdom, significance is the outcome of being sent. Your work is not in vain. What you call a waste of time on this mission I call a part of the plan. You would not understand the reason behind it, even if I were to explain it, until you have walked through it. Believe Me! There is no other choice. But you will be glad—soon.

I promise,

Dad

Struggling Child,

Humble yourself. I didn't say degrade yourself; I said humble yourself. You need faith. You are small, very small indeed. But your present situation is not as difficult as it appears—not if you can see your smallness and My greatness in it. Adopt this perspective and you will discover peace in this place where I have led you. Here, faith will abound and miracles must multiply. For you will have no one else to rely on but Me. Not even yourself.

How rarely these opportunities arise at this stage of your walk! But soon you will desire them, not dread them, because the glory of My power shines brightest in the absence of human help.

Always,

Dad

Frantic Fighter,

Tell Me. Be honest. Do you really have inner peace about this decision? Why do you fear the faces of men? Or the deadlines that people set? Am I not the Master Administrator? You know that I AM, child. I AM the Lord of time, and all times are subject to Me.

Has it not occurred to you that the Reason for all the sudden delays speaks to you even now? Why do you complain? Have a sense of adventure! You will like My plans far better than your own—or theirs.

Stop storming about and give no more place to the enemy! Hold fast to the peace I have given you. We all will be grateful if you will.

Love,

Dad

Ambitious Conqueror,

Jesus said, "You search the Scriptures, for in them you think you have eternal life, but they are that which testify of Me." So tell Me—are you searching the Scriptures to learn facts or to learn of Me?

I have called you to friendship, not frenzy. Life, not legalism! Child, seek to know Me, and in knowing Me you will know the truth as well, for truth transcends mere principle in the same way life transcends biological description. The Scriptures will help you to know Me, yes, but only if you meditate on them with a listening heart. Frankly, I have missed your singing lately.

Love,

Dad

Busy One,

Has it not yet occurred to you that I AM the One hindering your plans? Or perhaps I should say saving you from your plans? Come now! Whose gifts are you seeking to give, yours or Mine? And why?

Consider, cherished one. Can love and acceptance be bought? No, not in this world or any other. Take it from One who knows.

Had Jesus given His heart and His life for hurting humanity, expecting love to be returned in kind, then all would have been offered for naught. No, the very act of giving was joy enough.

You are right to believe that joy and giving are one. They are, if the giving finds its origin in My love. But for now, why not allow Me the joy of giving to you? I want to replenish your stores—to enlarge your capacity to bless others. Will you stand still long enough to allow Me to do so?

With all My Love,

Dad

Little One,

Of course not! I AM not angry with you for questioning. Can any sincere pursuit of knowledge offend Omniscience? Do you really believe your questions have estranged us? Never, child! It was I who said, "Come, let us reason together," was it not?

Now will you wait quietly, giving Me space to answer? Rudeness and haste are contrary to Kingdom policy, so I will not interrupt you. Further, I cannot always conform to your schedule. I love you too much.

Patiently,

Dad

Sorrowful One,

Death is forever swallowed up in victory! Receive My strength, child. I AM holding you. Despite the pain, I tell you truly—this is a chapter of new beginnings for you and your loved one. I AM mending your heart, and you will again know joy. Yes, unspeakable joy.

You are not wrong to trust Me, so be of good cheer. All will be well. Time and distance are not as your earthly eyes perceive them. Yes, beyond all human hope, and for now in a realm where only I can gain entrance, healing is flowing, I promise.

Yes, you will laugh together—again and again—and it will be in My presence that you do so.

Truly,

Abba

Cherished Child,

I choose to need you because I love you. I do not love you because I need you. I AM hoping My kind of love will overflow from you toward others.

What joy it is to have you with Me, imparting peace in our pressured world! People mangled by manipulation need us. As you walk in the light of My unfailing love, your radiance beams healing hope to many.

Wonderful!

Love,

Dad

P.S. Same message I just whispered in your spirit.

Chosen One,

Again, it has been My delight to hold you close, whisper My secrets in your ear, and joy in the wonder of you. I know. There are still some areas we both want to see healed, but those little pockets of pain have been inside you a very long time. And believe it or not, as troublesome as they are, to remove them all at once would be unwise. Through the years, little by little and deep within yourself, you came to think of those inner hurts as part of your identity. As a wise Master Builder I simply know that to replace those faulty parts with the original ones I designed for you does require a certain pace and process.

Why? You are always asking why, aren't you? But I have told you already! To heal those inner wounds in a single act of power would deny you the opportunity to grow, to know by experience, and thereby to become a compassionate deliverer. There are some kinds of knowing that only come by growing—otherwise why should My Son have arrived in your world as a baby?

Jesus Himself learned obedience—sinless though He was—by the things He suffered. Not even He was exempt. To fulfill all righteousness and lay hold of deepest wisdom, even Almighty God had to embrace pain and death. Christ's baptism into suffering and death has become your baptism into glory and life. How so!? Ha! Shall I send you a blueprint of the cosmos for starters? The full explanation lies beyond the range of mortal comprehension. At least, such is My view of the matter.

Trust Me! Do you have any other choice?

Tenderly,
Dad

Day 140

*First Kings 18:16-39;*
*Matthew 18:18-19*

Dear Child,

I know. You did all the right things. You examined your heart and repented. You prayed in agreement with My will as Scripture reveals it. You turned your attention away from the difficulty and directed your heart toward praise—continually. And you were faithful.

So why does the problem remain? Again, as a sovereign witness to My glory, I AM doing the manifestly impossible. As My fire fell upon the water-soaked altar at Mount Carmel and consumed the sacrifice, so shall I show My power yet again! Your change will come—be assured. But rest assured also that when it happens it will be a miracle. No one will dare be foolhardy enough to ascribe it to mere natural causes.

Thank you for waiting. Your patience for this witness will bring you rich reward!

Faithfully,

Abba

Willing Worker,

What comprises scriptural church government? One primary principle: Let the greatest among you become the servant of all. Will you help establish Heaven's government in your community?

Do what you wish, child! Forget all the stereotypes you've ever formed about "ministry." We need more carpenters, artists, technicians, and especially more willing workers advancing Our Kingdom. Real moms and dads are desperately needed.

Ever delighted to back you,

Dad

P.S. You're hearing Me right. Share the message! Boggle a mind. Win a heart.

# Day 142

My Worried Child,

Praise is the pathway to peace, as I have told you before. As you rejoice, I redeem; so cease all mental rehearsals of past reversals! Do you remember how I blessed and provided for young Ishmael despite the blunders of his father, Abraham? Abraham's blessings are yours, treasured one. Stop reasoning and ask! I have opened the windows of Heaven, and you need only to ask! Ask and ask and ask, for I delight to shower abundance upon you, causing your joy to inspire faith in the hearts of your friends.

I told you earlier of the harvest you would reap from those days of sowing in tears, did I not? Then ask. The harvest is ripe, and the day of your freedom has dawned! Today is the day of My power. Rejoice and be glad in it!

I AM!

Dad

Daring Deliverer,

Knowing why will never satisfy you like experiencing My power. This you have already discovered, but I just thought you would find a reminder refreshing.

Experience explodes arguments! Miracles unravel clever reasoning and spur people to re-evaluate their ideologies. Put on the mind of Christ, and dare to listen to your heart! Let's astonish a few doubters today—not excluding yourself.

I think you're wonderful.

Love,

Dad

Persistent Seeker,

Are you seeing it now? All the while you have been bombarding Heaven with prayers that seemed to go unanswered, I have been at work. All the while you were protesting and questioning, I was quietly healing, restoring, rearranging.

But you needn't feel guilty over the lashings of your flesh that have occurred in this process. Even these have worked for your good; they have deepened your capacity to understand My heart. For instance, you have learned a vital lesson about My sovereignty. Now you realize that the phrase "the sovereignty of God" is not an escape clause nullifying My promises. My sovereignty is your stronghold of security! Not only do I fulfill My commitments, but I do far, far above and beyond all you ask or think or imagine.

Yes. I do keep you guessing sometimes as to how I will answer your prayers, but that is because I AM a Person, not a principle to be manipulated. I AM faithful and reliable, but hardly predictable. Predictability is a characteristic of law and principle, not life and personality. Now you will sing "Great is Thy Faithfulness" and know what you are singing about! Yes?

How proud of your progress I AM!

Truly,

Abba

Indignant Disciple,

What? Not one of My children has ever paid his or her dues! Doesn't such thinking betray forgetfulness of Calvary?

People who demand to get what they "deserve" would be shocked if I gave it to them. As you know yourself, I have been known to use shock therapy as a last resort on occasions. Remember Jonah?

But thanks for leaving all emergency procedures to Me!

Abba

# Day 146

*Matthew 5:13;*
*Second Corinthians 10:12;*
*Ephesians 2:8-10*

Chosen Servant,

Why must you worry about the expectations of others? I have called you to be a prototype, not a stereotype—an original, not a copy. Child, you must not even try to fulfill human expectations, whether real or imagined! Not only is it a waste of time, it is a disservice to the very ones you would seek to please.

I have called you to be a deliverer—a savior—a champion! If you are to be what I have called you to be, you need to make pleasing Me your priority. Will you do that? I AM easier to please than you think, treasured one. All I ask is that you take time to receive My love, hear My voice, and dare to enact those tactics I share when we come together.

Of course, if you do, you are bound to seem radically different to certain ones at times. How well I know! Yet, if My truth is to be heard and My words are to penetrate, we often will need to challenge the "norms" of people. Good. If it has to be, then so be it. But be careful—don't start striving to be "different."

Don't seek uniqueness, and neither seek conformity. Seek Me. Always. Inquire of Me, and then listen to your heart. I will speak, and you will know it—and the fruit of your faith will show it. My peace will permeate your spirit, and quiet confidence will crown all you say and do. As you yield your heart to Mine, your actions will align with Mine, again and again, time after time. Then you will no longer try to be bold. No, obedience will build you to be bold.

Now will you forsake the futility of your frenzied planning? Rest! Shhh! Be quiet! I AM. Besides, I have already prepared the way.

Your Dad

Worried One,

Why should I object to doctors? I AM one! I often enrich My children by introducing them to My friends in the medical profession.

Trust Me to lead you. You are healed. All symptoms are fading. Beware of doubt and cynicism! Those devils lurk in the shadows of negative analysis, looking for ways to devour your joy.

Yours everlastingly,

Dad

*Galatians 6:9*

Delightful Child,

To your own eyes your works seem trivial and small, but not to Mine. Every extra mile and every menial task I have carefully noted, and your work has not been in vain.

Thank you for your diligence to help. And thank you for lightening the loads of My other children by doing those mundane tasks that many would choose to ignore. I have seen every sacrifice, every humiliation, and every heartache. You have borne the griefs of many less needy than yourself while suffering pains only I have known. Because you were faithful in small matters, I AM leading you into greater opportunities even now.

Very soon you will enter new joys and you will forget the present sorrow. Yes, all that was shattered will be mended and your pain will pass away. Again, child—you have not labored in vain.

Tenderly,

Dad

Questioning One,

As you know by now, I AM not One to waste words. If, at times, you hear nothing when you seek Me—rest! Abide in the strength of the previous words I have spoken. I often answer on a deeper level than language can express.

Child, in those moments you wait in My presence, what you call My silence is, in reality, My taking the opportunity to infuse you with new life. Every provision, every healing, and every solution springs from that quickening. When words are what you need, I will speak them.

Why must we always talk? Stay quiet, restless one! I have longed to hold you.

Gently,

Dad

Searching One,

What do you want? You have committed your way to Me. I have seen the surrender of your heart and I AM honoring your request that I guide you. Move with confidence! There is no chance of your veering off course.

Refuse to fret. What you choose I will choose! Even if some-how you were to choose a lesser good, you would still be in good hands—hands that are expert in turning smaller goods into greater ones. I AM the Master of time and events, so trust Me! I AM trusting you.

Isn't now as good a time as any for you to taste the joys of our reigning partnership? I think so. Step out! Be bold. We are des-tined to succeed, you and I. How could we possibly fail?

Committed in Love,

Dad

Psalm 24:1;
Isaiah 54:17;
Romans 11:6

Fatigued Freedom Fighter,

Identity determines desire, and desire gives birth to behavior. What is your identity? Do you know who you are? You will know who you are only when you know whose you are!

You are Mine. No weapon—again, I say—no weapon forged against you will prosper! Cease fretting, child. You yearn for My will, so you walk in My will. Legalism promotes uncertainty. Love fosters faith. My glory surrounds and shields you, and I love you!

Believe what I'm saying and no power can defeat you!

Dad

Searching One,

Am I not the Judge above all judges, the Attorney above all attorneys, and the King above all kings? I AM. Again, it is My joy to guard and protect you, and even now I AM scrambling the signals of the opposition. Soon every charge and technicality devised against you will vanish, so sing for joy!

Watch! I AM causing all carnal wisdom to crumble! Soon you will behold the befuddlement of your accusers and stand amazed as I contend with your contenders! Lost in the cloud of their own confusion, your enemies will grope blindly and they each will consume the other. You will see it with your very own eyes. Be assured, you will!

Will the courts of men be caught in the snare of their own craftiness? How could it be otherwise? Corruption can do nothing but invalidate itself, for deceit carries the seed of its own defeat, as I have told you before. Now will you be at peace? I AM.

Always,

Your Dad

*Psalm 32:1-2; 103:10-14;*
*Matthew 10:7-10*

Weary-Hearted One,

While you've been groveling and trying to atone for your sins, I've been maneuvering you into position to receive this message: *stop!* Please, tender one. Let's resume our adventure.

Apology accepted. Now forgive yourself. I forgive you—now go, not to get, but to give. I approve you, receive you, and delight to support you. Remember, you live, not for human applause, but to impart healing and hope.

Love always,

Dad

# Day 154

*Psalm 18; Matthew 20:28*

Questioning Conqueror,

I never promised you a path without resistance or an automatic deliverance that would demand no effort on your part. If you'll study the life of Jesus you will find it was the same with Him. He learned obedience through the things He suffered. In other words, obedience was woven into the fabric of the Son of Man by the same sharp needle of perseverance under pressure that you now encounter.

Do you suppose any prince preparing for his future kingship would ever be allowed to bypass basic training? Think about it. How would a commander lead an army unless he had submitted to the discipline of becoming a soldier himself? Should a man be made a company president if he has never learned the demands and details of the various departments of the business? Child, I bring this to your attention simply to remind you—the present pressures are not worthy to be compared with the glory I have prepared for you! Trust Me! But trust Me with tenacity and you will understand My purposes with conviction and clarity.

Believe Me, if you were unprepared for today's challenges I would have placed you elsewhere. All who would reign with Christ must share in His suffering and submit to His training. As you know, treasured child, in in My view, to reign means to serve. The Son of Man came not to be served, but to serve. So be assured; this is practice, not punishment. I AM preparing you for a destiny far higher than you ever dared imagine. Yes, I know. Some have betrayed and hurt you. I do understand your disappointment, child. If anyone understands, I do.

ABBA CALLING

173

Do you recall the fits of rage and attempted murder that My son, David, suffered at the hands of King Saul? And the stress he endured while fleeing for his very life? It was in those times I taught that man of My heart how to overcome evil with good, how to trust only in Me; and I gave him a far greater gift than ability. I gave him agility. And so it is with you. I AM giving you the feet of a deer so you may tread on precarious and slippery slopes with ease and delight. One day, glancing back from those exhilarating heights, today's trials will seem trifling in light of the transformation their training produced in you.

Of course, the real purpose of any valley through which you may pass cannot come into view until you reach sufficient height on the mountains to see with perspective. In the meantime, let us proceed through the foothills with joy!

Oh? You thought these were the mountains? Your tender feet are hardly ready for those yet, little one, but they will be soon enough, I assure you. I AM giving you beautiful feet—feet fit to run swiftly with the good news of My Kingdom. And I do know what I AM doing! Thank you for your trust.

Always, your Strong Fortress,

Dad

Tearful Rescuer,

I respect you. Therefore I grant you enormous freedom of thought and expression—even when you're dead wrong! Will you deny others the same freedom?

Sometimes Love must allow others to live with their choices. Is it merciful to deny people the wealth born of experience? Please, child. Learn to relax a little more, trusting My Holy Spirit! I will watch over your loved ones.

Yours tenderly and resourcefully,

Dad

Generous-Hearted One,

Yes, I agree. The grasping ingratitude and critical behavior of those around you was deplorable. And you are right. It seems nothing can please them.

But since you have been so frank in voicing your frustrations of late, I trust you'll not take offense from My being honest with you. I refuse to take the blame for these events! No, child, the fault lies with you. And I have protected you more than you know in the midst of your folly. When you helped them in the first place, you forgot to inquire of Me and wait for My answer.

But never fear—I AM working it out for your good. And please—trust Me as I deal with those who have hurt you. Sometimes I must allow people to come face to face with their lack to force them back to reality. But never mind. All will be well. You can call it a lesson learned by being burned.

Even so, be sure to forgive them—and yourself. You cannot afford not to. Actually, it was a fairly cheap education—considering all its benefits. Don't you agree?

Always seek Me first. You can count on Me to lighten your load and show you what is best. Only I can assess the truest needs of the heart. Sometimes I give My more stubborn children a far greater gift by refusing to yield to their demands. I love them enough to give them room to experience the end of their ways. Yes, as you know yourself, some come to their senses only when mounting expenses compel them at last to seek Me.

Always yours helpfully,
Dad

P.S. But of course I will meet all expenses, child. What are fathers for?

# Day 157

*Psalm 143:8-10;*
*Matthew 6:7-8; John 16:13;*
*Second Corinthians 4:6-7; Hebrews 4:16*

Cherished Searcher,

I AM here. Why are you shouting? I'm not deaf. I'm just waiting for you to finish talking.

Today, I AM training you to listen. Why are you looking here for guidance? Sing for joy! Then, listen to your own heart. Stop and listen! Heed your inner impressions. I inhabit your praises. Yes, that is where you will always discover Me as the *Living* God. And you are right—the hopes and hunches spurring you toward new ventures of faith are coming from Me. Hear Me, child. Hear Me out.

Yours, with all wisdom and power,

Abba

Zealous Disciple!

Untimely truth can be just as dangerous as outright error. You can avoid many pitfalls if you will keep this in mind. Think! Do earthly parents teach their children to play leapfrog before they have learned to walk? What would be the use of training an aspiring heart surgeon in the field of cosmetology? Child, good educators present a curriculum based upon many factors, including the age, abilities, and gifts of their students. Am I not as wise?

Any truth I intend for you will always be timely, helpful, and liberating; it will never produce frenzy or despair. Information is not education; ill-timed, it brings disorientation. Will you please trust My timing? Eat only the food I set before you! When in doubt, ask! Wait! If at times some of My more exuberant children share their lessons with you, then you must recognize them as being just that: their lessons. And rejoice with them in their new discoveries while remembering this: you are required to fulfill only the assignments I have given to *you*.

Trust Me. You can rely on My promises. Enjoy your life. As you do, My anointing will teach you all you need to know.

In joy!

Your Dad

Searching Deliverer,

I know you are like Me in your yearning to see real love released to heal a needy world, so let Me guide you in your giving. If all My children learned to do that, institutions that oppress in My name would either purge themselves or disappear!

Love is patient. Just follow Me. Refuse to let any person or power intimidate you. Don't worry about what you don't have to give. Give what you have. I evaluate one's giving by what one has. I never judge by what one does not possess.

Remember this. I AM Love. You have Me, and I have you.

Always!

Dad

# Day 160

Little One,

It is no trouble to tell you again; "...as the heavens are higher than the earth, so are My thoughts higher than yours!" You have not been wrong to question. You have just been asking the wrong questions. The enemy always clouds the real issues, don't you remember? Diversion is his oldest trick. But in answer to your question—no. Your problems are not My punishment. I never repay evil for evil, nor do I treat people as their sins deserve.

Actually, it is not a matter of deserving anything, good or bad. The real issue is the imperishable seed of My Word, for My Word is an inseparable extension of My essence and life. I and My Word are one! So when will you believe in Me? I AM the Seed of Abundant Life and I contain all the fruit you have longed to harvest. But remember, a seed can only sprout if it remains planted. Isn't observing a seed the exact opposite of planting one? Yes, the seed of My Word must stay buried in the soil of faith if it is ever to grow.

Keep My Word planted in your heart! Cease looking at outward appearances. Decide now, child. Are you going to view this situation through earthly eyes or through the eyes of faith? Is seeing believing? No, cherished one. Believing is seeing—truly seeing!

If you will stop rationalizing and start rejoicing in My great love for you, you will see what I mean.

Truly,

Dad

# Day 161

Self-Searching Child,

I know it hasn't been easy for you. But their problem is not your problem—not unless you insist on making it yours! Relish rest. You need it.

Rest in My love. Savor serenity. You are not playing games with My grace. If you were, I would be the first one to tell you.

Heaven applauds your patience!

Abba

Cherished Conqueror,

Growing up is never easy. Each new stage of growth from infancy to adulthood requires that you leave what is comfortable and familiar and embrace the unknown and uncharted.

So this means that I cannot always carry you if you are to discover the joy of walking, nor can I go on spoon-feeding you if you are ever to learn how to feed yourself. So, in a sense, you are right. Lately I have "distanced" Myself from you in certain ways so that in more important ways I can bring us closer together. I do this, not to desert you, but to give you opportunity to grow. In growing, you will discover an intimacy and closeness between us that never could have been possible had I dealt with you as I did earlier. As a full-grown son learns to know the heart of his father far beyond the limited understanding he had as a toddler, in the same way I'm training you to know Me now.

So, for a time it will seem as though I'm farther away, but the very reason I created you was so that you could enjoy My friendship to the fullest and reign with Me! For that to happen, you must learn to stand on the two feet I have given you. And you also must learn to trust My Spirit who lives inside you.

Now be honest. Do you think you would put any real effort into learning these things if I were to go on hovering over your every move as I did in earlier years? I think we both know the answer to that. Trust Me! I know what I'm doing and you're going to like it.

Always!

Dad

# Day 163

Curious Conqueror,

Far be it from Me to refuse your requests! Trust Me, child. I have called you and I will perfect all that concerns you. I AM the God of covenant faithfulness and I AM committed to you. I will perform all I have promised. And yes, your desires align with My wisdom and design, so cease questioning the validity of your prayers.

Haven't I promised that if you ask anything according to My will, that I have heard you, and you have the things you've desired of Me? I remind you—My will is My Word, and My Word is My will. They are one and the same. So let nothing steal your joy. Even now I AM doing abundantly above and beyond all you have asked or imagined.

Late! Since when was I ever late?

Confidently,

Dad

Annoyed Seeker,

Yes, you are absolutely right. I have heard your request, but I AM doing what I prefer to do anyway! Have you thought about how often My "stubbornness" has saved you?

I know. You cannot understand what I AM doing right now. But you will understand later on. Trust Me! I AM leading you into deliverance, not destruction. You are My handiwork, My creation, My treasure!

Yours with eternal devotion!

Dad

# Day 165

*Matthew 6:3-4;
John 12:25-26*

Faithful Servant,

Even now, I AM rewarding you for the long hours you have spent revealing My heart to My needy children. I AM multiplying back to you the gifts you have given. I know. Many have been thoughtless where your needs are concerned. Even so, thank you for your generosity to help and comfort them.

Shall I tell you why I sent you on this mission? Child, you are one of the few—one of the very few—who is willing to work without the guarantee of short-term rewards. Many give readily enough to the destitute, helpless, and impoverished. But rarely can I find one willing to love the immature and ungrateful who have not yet learned to give in return. Sadly, many of My co-laborers are prone to judge by the outward appearance. They fail to see the desperate poverty beneath the façade worn by those who appear to be more affluent.

Mere decency demands giving to the obviously poor, but who will humble himself to the thankless task of serving the merchants, tax collectors, and publicans? You happen to be one of the few, child.

Be prepared. Some will question the abundant gifts I will soon lavish upon you publicly. When they do, just tell them it was My idea, and it had to do with some secret projects we have shared. If they are really troubled about it, I would be more than happy for them to take it up with Me.

Yours proudly!

Dad

# Day 166

Second Corinthians 4:6-7;
Ephesians 1:15-23; 5:8-11

Trusted Trooper,

Light exploded! Pulsating radiance showered, surrounding the tomb. Then, two thunderbolts struck the earth and snapped into the shape of angels! Awestruck, the soldiers guarding the crypt fled. Your Lord emerged, smiling. And you think of resurrection power as just theological rhetoric? Have I got surprises for you!

I created you to conquer. Just remember who you are! View every trial as an invitation to experience the miraculous—as a door opening into supernatural exploits of power!

All sufficiently yours,

Dad

Fretful Helper,

Again, you simply must commit your failures and those of all others to Me. Trust Me to finish the work of your salvation—and theirs. Leave all end results to Me. You have already discovered that the flesh is powerless to conquer the flesh. Only *by My Spirit* can you put to death the deeds of the flesh and live. Not by might, nor by power, but by My Spirit! A magnificent way to live, isn't it?

Think of it this way. A good lawn is more the result of planting seeds than pulling weeds. It is the same in the Heavenly realm. If the good seeds are sown and nourished, they will produce a thick carpet of grass that will choke out most of the weeds.

Here is the working principle: you plant the seeds, and I will pull the weeds. Plant them by walking in the joy of My promises! And encourage your loved ones. Today commit yourself to becoming a continuous encourager. Look for the praiseworthy! Engender an environment of encouragement. This will release the revelation that only hearts united by love can receive. Then you will see the answers to your prayers for your loved ones.

Love them as they are, for that is how Christ loves you, cherished one. It is also how I love you.

Talk about transforming power! Right?

You know I AM,

Abba

Tender Restorer,

Exhibit honesty and integrity, yes. Adopt a policy of whole-sale transparency with all people? No!

Those who look to illusions for happiness resent anyone desecrating their idols. I don't want others ripping you to shreds when you're already hurting. Lean on Me! I will deal with those who want you to replace Me for their pleasure.

I love you too much to let others mistake you for Me. Aren't you glad?

Love,

Dad

Day 169

*Isaiah 50:4; Jonah 2:6;*
*Matt 12:40; Romans 8:17*

Questioning One,

Why do you doubt? Have I ever failed to give you wisdom or direction when you have asked? I have put My words in your mouth and covered you with the shadow of My hand. None of our words can fail, for My Spirit has anointed your tongue with wisdom to comfort the weary.

There is a time for reaping, but bear in mind that reaping always follows the time for planting. Be encouraged! I AM with you. You haven't spoken wrong or useless words. Give Me time to water the seeds of truth we have planted in the hearts of My children. Remember My principle of process. Sometimes it seems to you that My process drags on *forever,* I know. It seemed the same to Jonah, as well. Later he discovered that his "eternity" of trouble had lasted but three days.

Even Jesus did not always receive immediate results. Often His words were simply rejected. He is your Example, your Teacher; you cannot be greater than He. Rest! You do not see all of the picture. You see only a part of it, so cheer up! Return to joy. I have not called you to produce ready-made results. I have called you to bear fruit, and bear it you will, in My appointed time. A great harvest of blessing is coming! I promise.

Forever,

Your Dad

Psalm 18:31-34; 62:1-2;
Proverbs 2:8; Hebrews 13:8

Anxious One,

Are you running scared? Trembling? Covering bases? Rehearsing defenses? Stop! My glory shields you, and My love secures you, little one. I will not abandon you. When all systems fail, you still have a Fail-Safe System.

No one is wasting your time. I interrupted your schedule for a progress report. You look ten years younger with your pulse rate back to normal!

Rest in My embrace,

Abba

*Philippians 3:13-15*

Sorrowful One,

About those regrets—surely you know they are forgiven? It would be wiser now, if you think of them at all, to see them as stepping stones toward knowledge. It is a waste to think of them in any other way, for I turn all regrets into resources.

Have you thought of this? To emphasize your failures is actually to de-emphasize My power! Also, it is to magnify your own significance where the happiness of others is concerned. Child, I alone can bestow happiness for I AM the Source of Joy! Only when people experience My nurture and friendship can they be truly happy. In My fellowship, they will experience a serenity that can hardly be challenged, even when others mistreat them.

But understand. I AM not excusing or speaking lightly of selfish behavior. Selfish acts are sin, and sin cannot be simply excused. It must be confessed, repented of, forgiven, and cleansed. Repentance is the only real solution for sin.

But this has not been the need in your case. You grieve over sins long ago forgiven. The enemy tortures you. He tells you that your stumblings have brought excessive grief to others. It is a lie, tender-hearted child. There is no damage I cannot repair or wound that I cannot heal. Besides, I have not commissioned you to assure the happiness of other people. You have only one commission, and that is to trust in Me.

Will you trust Me? Remember, trusting, like any other action, is a choice. And while you are making choices, will you also make this one—choose to forgive yourself! Self-inflicted punishment can do nothing to alter the past, and continuing remorse is of no value at all. Forgiveness means you are free from your yesterdays—forever! So will you simply enjoy My love again and go on sharing it with others?

And child, thank you for being willing to go the second mile. Well done.

Love,

Dad

Mighty Conqueror,

You will remain happy if you will bear in mind that reigning with Christ means nurturing, healing, and serving. Sometimes you will suffer, especially at the hands of people who are in charge of abusive religious systems. However, that will remind you that reigning with Christ *does not* mean "lording it over" those whom I have called you to love and heal. A lost and deluded world reigns by intimidation and control, yes. The same is true of a lost and misguided church! But of course, everyone knows that. What else is new?

Child, just remember that I have called *you* to conquer by Love—Love that never fails! And thus you will—and must—conquer, for Unfailing Love is who I AM.

I'm *so* blessed having you in My life! I mean that.

Your devoted Dad

Searching Child,

Surely by now you have learned the folly of forcing a closed door? A forced entry always begets an unhappy ending. Many doors will appear in your lifetime, but not all of them will be yours. And even those that are yours must be entered at the proper time and in the proper way. Any door that would seem to require force should become an occasion for you to inquire of Me. I have set before you an open door. Remembering this will spare you further stress.

Cease remorse and stop trying to analyze your recent blunders. All is forgiven. As I see it, your tenacity is actually one of your more delightful qualities. I just want to help you put it to better use.

Affectionately,

Dad

Restless Runner,

Why do you fear opening your heart to Me? I have *no desire whatsoever* to hinder your happiness. But I will say, what you sometimes call "happiness" I call only a clownish copy of joy. Child, I alone can give substance to your hopes, your desires, and your dreams, but that is the discovery you have yet to make.

So often you shrink back from Me for fear of loss or unreasonable demands when, in reality, I ask for all of your heart to make possible your having all of Mine. When we each possess the other's heart, you will clearly see that there can be no conflict of interests. Just to confirm what your spirit has been hearing...

Patiently, tenderly,

Dad

Faithful One,

The time you spend with Me is never wasted; for though you have not known it, your prayers ascend as incense before Me. Why do you imagine that I question your love? Your constant return to My Presence surely proves otherwise. Each time you pause to hear My voice, even if you are unaware of it, a new miracle is seeded within you. Haven't you discovered this by now? Of course you have. Rest in this knowledge! Your miracle will arrive when needed, but let the seed now take root in the ground. And live one day at a time. Do you really have any choice?

Faithfully,

Abba

# Day 176

1 Kings 17:7-14;
Psalm 25:15;
John 11:1-44

Diligent Child,

I repeat. Look only where I instruct you to look, and trust Me to lead you. Discover and savor the serenity that defies reason, the peace that permeated the heart of Jesus. That peace empowered Him to heed My still, small voice despite the desperate demands that came from the family of His dying friend, Lazarus. Lay hold of the bold faith of Elijah, who, in obedience to My word, instructed the widow of Zaraphath to prepare her last morsel of meal to feed him.

I will give you an unearthly calm that no storm, no fiery furnace, and no contradiction can challenge if you will look only to Me. But again—you must look only to Me. I will lead you in the way you should go and I will contend with every enemy. Haven't I recently shown you this? You know that I have. Cease teetering on a tightrope, between two opinions. Pursue peace, child. I will perfect your path!

With joy!

Abba

Struggling Restorer,

The law is but a verbal description and a dim reflection of the way My divine life appears when you see it in action. This is true of the Law of Moses and it is also true of the law of Christ, as expressed in the Sermon on the Mount. So will you please stop trying to produce a virtuous life by frantic self-effort? Apart from Me you can do nothing. You cannot manufacture real life; My Spirit must bring it to birth.

You cannot love your friends, let alone your enemies, unless you receive My life-giving nurture. Jesus said that a good man speaks from the good stored up in his heart. Do you recall? Your heart is a tired and empty one. Allow Me to fill it.

And never fear. The radiant light of My love from within you will reconcile your enemies or else repel them. Either way, you'll not find them a problem. Believe Me.

Abba

Holy Helper,

I enjoy the scenario of theater and costume as much as anyone does! But does reverence consist of donning old-fashioned clothes, talking shoddy Shakespearean, and tiptoeing about in cadence with organ music? Ha! Thou waxeth too old to buy into that blarney.

Holiness overlooks crude words and loves people! It scorns the somber sanctimony and sham of religion. True holiness laughs! Love people! Eschew pomposity.

Through your love and laughter, can your fellow workers even detect that I like them?

Yea, verily!

Thy Dad

Questioning Child,

I really can be trusted. Do you honestly believe I would ignore you in the hour of your greatest need? Peace. I AM arranging events even now to release you from those inner struggles and conflicting demands, and your release will come quite apart from your own strength or striving.

This deliverance will not be as stressful as you have imagined, for the worst is already past. Will you rest in Me? The happiness of your loved one is also assured, for I joined you together. My grace covers and secures you both.

Why do you imagine yourself unworthy? I have come to the sick, not the well. Child, groveling in remorse will never cure any weakness or produce any good, so shall we leave the past in the past where it belongs?

Cease all frantic self-scrutiny, please, dear child. Focusing on your faults cannot cure them. Putting yourself down will never elevate your spirit. I created you to conquer, and conquer you will! How so? Jesus destroyed sin and death when I raised Him back to life, and you came to life with Him. From My eternal point of view, Christ's life made all things new.

From your finite point of view, your new life has barely begun. Be patient. I AM. I see you as you really are—eternally in Christ—all the time. You are discovering your true self, moment by moment, day by day—and that's okay. I have all your lapses covered. Love covers a multitude of lapses.

Interesting provisions are coming soon—seemingly out of nowhere. They will arrive perfectly timed to meet all needs. And there will even be supply for some of your little wants—those secret desires of your heart, which I have known, though you have never dared to voice them to Me. Pardon My eavesdropping, but being what and who I AM, it was unavoidable!

Tenderly,

Abba

Child of My Heart,

Why are you waiting on Me? I AM waiting on you! The sound of your voice delights Me. I like hearing you talk. When you pray, why do you wrestle with words, cherished one? It is the accuser who nitpicks with your vocabulary, not I. I AM hearing your heart.

I will tell you again. I don't mind telling you again and again—and yet again. *I like you.* That does a number on your theology, doesn't it? Good!

Always!

Your Dad

# Day 181

My Dear Child,

I think you're wonderful. You have amazing spiritual sensitivity. You really do. When will you trust your own ability to hear Me? Why do you look for fire, thunder, and a strange voice resonating from the beyond? Why do you depend upon other listeners?

Trust Me to guide your heart. What do you think I might be saying in those moments when you listen for My voice? When you seek My counsel, choose to heed the words and receive the impressions I give you. Stop attributing them to your own imagination. Why are you surprised that My thoughts "feel" like your own? They are! I gave them to you.

When you ask for a good gift, even if the gift you seek is a word from Me, believe in My integrity. Write down what comes to your mind as you wait before Me. Write the vision and make it as plain as possible. I will confirm all I have said in the hours to follow.

Why don't I speak louder, you ask? Shouting in the house is just not a habit of Mine. Please—allow Me to be Myself with you. Let Me be natural. Shouldn't the Lord of the "supernatural" be the most natural of all?

Helpfully,

Dad

Inquiring Child,

All I do, I do in your best interest. In fact, I love you so much that I often look beyond your small requests and give you far better gifts than you ask Me to give. I do supremely above all you ask or think. And why? You are a member of My royal family, and I think you deserve the best! So will you stop fretting about those "unanswered" prayers? I AM giving you what you really want—not what you think you want. Do you mind?

Frankly, you're not asking for too much, but for too little. I've hesitated to respond to your requests for this reason. Quiet your heart in My Presence, and reassess your requests! I long to lavish you with abundance.

Cheerfully,

Dad

Heavy-Hearted One,

Why did I allow you to suffer betrayal? Now you know how never to treat a friend. I trusted you in that trial.

Anything you long to express, I long to hear. Or you can just cry as I hold you in My arms, if you want to. My all-knowing heart needs no explanation.

This pain soon will cease, I promise. The enemy is doomed to defeat. We will win! Hide and watch.

With deepest compassion,

Abba

Bewildered Child,

If you ever begin to feel that you have no further need to grow, beware. Complacency is toxic and leads to paralysis. Godliness with contentment is indeed great gain, and no one knows that better than I. Yet may I tell you the vital difference between contentment and complacency? A contented man cares, whereas a complacent man coasts.

Child, you know I AM Perfect Rest personified, but I never coast passively through life. I AM constantly scanning all creation with searching eyes, looking for ways to bless and to impart joy! And what is joy? Often it is easier to see what a thing is if at first you see what it is not, so I will put it this way.

Any joy dampening the desire to grow, or to give is a delusion and a counterfeit. Any professed holiness dulling the spirit to the hurts of a dying world is not holiness, but hardness of heart. Any success or joy attained that imparts the "warm and fuzzy feeling" that you no longer need to lean on Me is delusional. True joy energizes. False joy paralyzes. It always leads to grief.

Child, I delivered you once from those dark desires of your earlier years—gladly. But I freed you, not to parade you about as a religious mannequin of moral purity. No, My heart was to fill you with My passionate joy! I longed for the real you, the "you" that only Jesus, My Gift of Life, could call forth! The last thing I wanted was a walking, talking "spiritual zombie."

Now do you see why those old feelings have begun creeping back? The reason they came in the first place was because you walked apart from Me, feeling pressured to become something you could not. Do you remember? Those old fantasies were your only escape.

Why not take the Great Escape? Repent. In other words, scamper back to sanity, child! You've not lost as much ground as you think. I made certain to get you this message before you did.

Love,

Dad

Hesitant Warrior,

Wisdom and direction granted! No longer hesitate, but step out with the confidence of a conqueror. How amazed you will be to see how easily all factors fall into line! You will wonder how you ever could have questioned.

Your times are truly in My hands, even as were Sarah's. Do you recall how I prepared her body for the birth of Isaac by reversing the ravages of time? Sarah, being well-advanced in years, was so obviously restored to her youth that a king once contemplated adding her to his harem, though he did so much to his court's inconvenience. Review the story for yourself, and remember—the same God is walking with you. Truly, I AM.

Your Abba

Perplexed Perfectionist,

You lived on earth about a year before you began toddling. Do you think I expect you to sprout wings and soar with angels by next summer? I AM pleased with your progress! Let's enjoy each other.

Please don't allow remorse to drive you away from Me. How could I be disappointed with you? I foresaw your struggles, your growing-pains, long before you were born. Better times are ahead! Refuse to delay them with despair.

Loving you always,

Dad

Frustrated Child,

Why do you keep fretting about those little wants of yours? All your life you have feared that I would supply only your bare physical necessities. You have thought My promise to meet all of your needs meant that I would give you nothing else. I ask you! Does a loving earthly father so strictly ration his children?

I know. There are some somber ones who view almost all things as either vain or frivolous. Why do you keep listening to those who think they are more spiritual than I AM? Things, especially physical things, are neither good nor bad in or of themselves. I've certainly never had a problem with them.

Of course, as a loving and responsible Father, I withhold from you those things I know would waste your time or bring you pain. For your own sake, I do for you what you would want done, if you but knew all end results. In the meantime, I go on giving you My best gifts. And My best gifts have a quality about them that causes you to grow and mature toward more discerning tastes.

Be patient! Do you remember some of the things you thought you wanted and thought you couldn't live without five years ago? Aren't you glad now that they failed to materialize? Recall the great relief My stubbornness and practicality have brought you—many times, to say nothing of My amazing timing!

Still fighting for you, cheerfully,

Abba

Loving Little One,

Israel once longed for a king; being wearied of My government, My people envied to be as other nations. I sorrowed for them. I knew what they desired would bring them far more pain than happiness. Yet, in the end, I granted their request, for they could learn no other way. And since having an earthly kingdom was better than having none at all, I gave them the kingdom they thought they wanted. They could have had Mine.

Will you learn from them? I desire a more excellent way for you. Receive My greater gifts. Trust Me! You will see that I do have all your interests and happiness at heart. In fact, within these next few weeks and even in the next seven days, you will see Me provide—in microscopic detail—many of those little wants you have expressed.

By the way, you are in for some surprises. You have forgotten that you even asked for some of the things you are about to receive. You forgot, but I did not. Haven't I shown you that you need not always ask Me directly? That I delight to surprise you with the little things? Things that you mention to others or just simply wish? You know I have.

Soon you will be older and know Me better and then you will strive angrily against Me less. You have exhausted yourself with shadow-boxing, child. I AM not against you. I AM for you! How I long for the day when you discover how much I greatly delight in you.

Always,
Dad

Recovering Child,

A bruised reed I will not break; a smoldering candle I will not snuff out.

Jesus is the Light of Life; therefore, My Son perfectly reflects My nature! Why do you tremble in fear that I will desert you? I AM working to fulfill your dearest dreams—to heal you, not to abuse you.

You may as well decide never to give up on Me. Whatever you do, I will never give up on you. Make it easy on yourself! Everlasting Love just doesn't know how to quit. One day you'll understand. You are destined to become as I AM.

Tenderly,

Abba

Child,

When you seek Me for guidance, do you delight in the "revelation" I give you more than you delight in our friendship? Is your joy more rooted in the fact that you have heard Me speak than in putting into practice the things you have heard Me say? This is a common trap, and I want you to be aware of it.

This is why lately I have withheld My revelations, My supernatural acts. If at this point I were to go on showering miracles and manifesting My power, I would be conducting a mere magic show—a performance to be connoisseured and critiqued.

I have better things in mind for you. I want you to know Me and understand My heart. Nothing less can make you truly happy. Never fear, I have no intention of ceasing to supply your needs. Miracles will come; I just want to direct your focus away from mere things and toward the Source from which they come.

One day, when it dawns on you how much I really love you, you will love Me without reservation or question. Not that you will cease asking questions, of course. That's not in My heart at all. Your relentless quest for truth always delights Me.

Sincerely,

Abba

Busy One,

I know it seems a senseless waste of time to come aside and commune with Me when there is so much to be done—especially for an active "doer" like yourself. I'm also aware of the struggles you have with guilt feelings when you do make time for those quiet moments.

Isn't it interesting how the enemy suddenly starts harping about "practicality" and "the need for good time management" when you are taking time for us? Amazing!

Dear child, if you have him worried, you must be on the right track! Stop fretting and keep investing in our friendship. The moments spent with Me have already saved you far more time than you know.

Truly,

Dad

Faithful Conqueror,

Now do you see it? Everything, literally everything you commit to My trust I redeem and return to you multiplied! It was hard going there for a while, but reaching the end of yourself did put you in reach of Something greater, did it not?

Obedience is better than sacrifice, as the recent restorations obviously show. Yes, entrusting your loved ones to Me, you will be happier with the outcome—always. Remember, Kingdom wisdom never worries, and mountains are moved by Mercy, not manipulation. Will you teach this to the children?

Thanks again!

Abba

Determined Law Enforcer,

"It's not the money; it's the principle! It's not their odd and frumpy clothing; it's the principle! It's not that I'm a racist; it's the principle! I'm not judging; it's just the principle!"

Intolerance, hatred, bigotry, envy, and greed find enormous satisfaction in preaching "principles." I AM not impressed. Are you?

How will people who are fearing punishment and scrambling to survive ever find time to recognize love, let alone receive or transmit it? Threats and fault-finding spawn paranoia. Paranoia breeds hate and intolerance, not holiness! Whose kingdom are you promoting?

Committed to Good News, always!

Abba

*First Corinthians 2:7-16; 6:17*

Courageous Conqueror,

I AM for you, I AM with you, and I AM in you. You have heard My words, beheld My acts of deliverance, and seen My wisdom at work repeatedly. My power rests upon you and the mind of Christ saturates your spirit.

So why are you seeking mere scraps of information again? My character and heart have permeated your own more than you have dared to believe. I repeat: speak and you will see. Go and you will know!

Stop depending on formulas and regulations! Use the eyes of your heart. Dare to say and do what you see Me saying and doing. Do what you believe Jesus would do were He doing it Himself! Then you will discover that He is—through you.

Put on the mind of Christ! Then do as He did. Start speaking words that sound like Mine and start taking steps that look like Mine, and you will find that all your acts will be Mine, I promise. What have you got to lose? I think we've both noticed you're not very good at rule-keeping.

Honestly but affectionately,

Dad

Inquiring Child,

Life without Love...is it possible? I have never thought so. What do you think? I AM Love. But some of My children think I'm narrow-minded and old-fashioned and they have set out to prove Me wrong.

I will tell you what I think. If you never learn anything else, what I want most for you is that you learn to love. In loving and truly caring about others you will acquire a wisdom that will never fade with your years. Riches will come to you that no earth-wealth can rival, and—best of all—you will be happy.

Are you amazed that God wants you to be happy? Why shouldn't I? I AM the Best Friend you will ever have!

Yours with infinite joy,

Your Dad

Matthew 6:22-23;
James 3:13

Faithful One,

Have you noticed how hypocrites can always spot other hypocrites? Nothing delights a hypocrite more than exposing another's flaws.

Some people prefer being "right" to being healed. I have plopped you in the midst of such madness to function as a stabilizer—not to speak or expound, but simply to be the blessing you are.

People who forget your extra efforts aren't ungrateful; they're just more secure, having you around! Thank you for showing love, kindness, and mercy.

With deepest gratitude,

Dad

Eloquent Liberator,

I chuckle as I say this, but what are you telling Me that I do not already know? All of your deepest longings lie open before Me. When you cease talking, I will speak. Meanwhile your monologue is delaying our dialogue.

Don't misunderstand Me, child. I AM not unhappy that you are pouring out your heart to Me. I just want you to know that I AM here for you, and that I care, and that you *can* hear Me speaking inside you—when you are ready.

You have asked that I not let you stray from My will. I AM answering your prayers. So why do you fret? I AM granting you wisdom, protection, and guidance, as per your request. Now, what do *you* want? Think about it. I'll be delighted to help you survey your options—in detail.

Do you fear hearing My heart? You shouldn't. When did I ever abuse or deprive you? Again, child, all I AM doing is answering your prayers. Whatever you choose to do, I assure you that you will be glad later on that you took time to become quiet in My Presence.

No, I AM not annoyed. Not at all. When I created you I knew that sometimes you would be a bit...challenging? I love everything about you.

Your Devoted Abba

Loveable Inquirer,

Although many seem to ignore Jesus, in their heart of hearts they aren't opposed to the Real Jesus. They are simply rejecting a warped presentation or concept of Him.

Jesus carried your sorrows. He bore your wounds, absorbing your sins and their dread harvest into His innocence. His stripes replaced the searing pain of your sickness with His wholeness.

This is just to confirm what you already know but sometimes forget. Fret not. Spiritual awakening is coming! Corrupt religiosity is going!

With love everlasting,

Dad

Cherished Seeker,

I have heard your prayers, so be assured—you will shine! Without conscious thought you will transmit the healing radiance of My Glory. Just abide in My loving nurture and Presence. You do not need mere information; you need who I AM.

Yes, you'll have to think about that, won't you? Good! Meditate on it. Yes! You need who I AM! Furthermore you already have Me right here with you. No earthly wealth can begin to rival the riches you possess!

Like yourself, Moses yearned that I show him My glory, and I fulfilled his longing—freely. Do I show favoritism? Do I love my son Moses more than you? Certainly not! He wrestled with frailties just as you do, yet I did what he asked, just because I wanted to.

Treasured conqueror, as I was with Moses, so I will be with you. Seek and you *shall* find.

With joy everlasting,

Your Devoted Abba

Lonely Warrior,

It's hard always having to be right, isn't it? Your friends and loved ones would enjoy you more if being right made you less abrasive and more pleasant. No one has the nerve to pass you this message. So, as usual, I have to be the "bad guy."

No. I never grow tired of hauling you out of ditches. You're the one who becomes weary, not I. I do look forward to your enjoying another lifestyle, cherished one. Soon you'll become tired enough of this one to opt for a new one.

Ever devoted to your joy,

Abba

Trusted Nurturer,

Yes, I have taught you well. Thank you for holding fast to that which is good. I also appreciate your generosity in sharing with others all that I have lavished on you. However, you are now beginning to realize that what I have taught you thus far is not enough. It is true, weary one. What you know has value only as it leads you to enter into who I AM and into experiencing the wonder of who I'm shaping you to be.

You have asked, "Why do I still worry so much?" I will tell you. You need love, not just correct concepts about it. You need hope—solid and real hope—not mere explanations as to why it is possible. There will never come a time when Love will fail. People fail, but I never do. My Only Begotten Son came to help and to heal failing people. Have you forgotten? As long as you imagine that I want you to be miserable, you will be. You will never love Me, nor will you ever trust Me wholeheartedly, until you *know* that I love you more, far more, than you love Me.

I AM unfailing Holy Love. Until unfailing Holy Love becomes all in all—everything in everyone everywhere—pain will persist in your world. Therefore, the more My Essence saturates your being, the more deeply you will know contentment. I created you for My delight. Do you remember? You were made for infinite joy!

Enter in, child. Taste and see! Perfect Love casts out all fear. Worry will vanish! All problems will lose their power to harass you in the secret place of the Most High. Treasured child, why should I be angry because I have waited for you? I have waited for you all of My life!

With deepest joy,
Your Dad

Browbeaten Child,

Do you want to know how to nudge chronic critics over the edge? Dare to smile kindly and remain silent! Reply only if I clearly lead you to speak. Jesus often did this, and did He raise a ruckus! Redemption resulted.

When criticized, receive it as an opportunity to perceive the pain of another's heart. If guilty, repent. If not, rejoice that Jesus trusted you to share in His suffering and Mine. I know all about you, and I AM still here. Doesn't this say anything to you?

Helpfully,

Dad

Searching One,

As you have noticed, I never rush. Nor am I ever bored (except with sundry religious affairs), and I never feel nervous or tense. The longer we walk and talk together, and the more you allow Me to embrace you and enjoy your company, the less nervous and tense you will be. More and more you will become as I AM. You will increasingly think as I think, feel as I feel, and live as I live. That is My commitment to you. You can count on it.

The constant and gentle impact of My Presence on your life has a "rubbing-off effect." The more you are exposed to My Essence, the more My nature rubs off on you. Little by little and bit by bit, who I AM frees you to become who you are—who you actually are. But this process *must* occur gradually, here a little, there a little.

A doctor doesn't use an atomic bomb to perform radiation therapy. Such treatment would annihilate his patient, not heal him. So aren't you glad that I AM not in a hurry? You can relax now. I AM your Physician, and I will not fail. And neither will you. It is not going to happen. So you may as well choose not to worry.

I AM like the sign you have seen written on the rear of those large transport trucks that says: *I may be slow, but I am ahead of you.*

Chosen conqueror, mere words cannot describe how much I enjoy your company.

Dad

Tortured Child,

Those dark daydreams that rage in your mind are not yours. Why should I be angry with you? Those lying illusions come from the enemy! He's hoping to make you forget who you are. Child, sometimes you may forget, but I never will. Not in a million eternities! Not ever!

Your mighty fortress,

Abba

Patient Restorer,

Thank you for your passion to love and serve others even when they fail to notice or show appreciation. Rejoice in My embrace. Spend the rest of this day basking in My enjoyment of you. In childlike trust, look for Me in all, and you will see Me in all. You will see Me in all situations, all events, all encounters.

Haven't I promised that even if you grow weary or stumble I will never forsake you? I have recently shown you, yet again, that your security does not depend on your own energy, wisdom, or efforts. It is My power that sustains, guides, and protects you. Always!

I want you to savor *every* joy and succeed in *every* good venture. However, you cannot wholeheartedly obey Me and thus experience these blessings as long as you labor under the illusion that your behavior or success determines My commitment to you. That is the lie of conditional love. As long as you believe that lie, despair and frustration will dominate your life. True righteousness arrives—and thrives—in an environment of joy. Focusing on problems will never free you from their power. Redirect your focus, treasured conqueror, toward Someone who loves you far more than you can imagine.

Your Devoted Abba

Ruthless Reasoner,

If your brain cells evolved from random atomic microparticles colliding in an irrational universe, why does your rational mind detest other such collisions like mass genocide, torture, and stealing? Did a cosmic "accident" produce those marvels called human reason and conscience? Couldn't resist asking!

Ever pursuing you,

Abba

Hurting Child,

I have come so that your fears will go away. Perfect Love—that is My name. In My Presence no fear can survive. Our being together now is no coincidence. Those lies luring you into despair are satanic. Reject them! That which is Holy inspires hope. The slippery serpent accuses and slanders. He is the one who trumps up fictitious scenarios to torment your mind. It is he who seeks to paralyze you. Why? That wicked one knows the power you wield. He knows the divine energy that surges inside you, which you have yet to discover. So of course he invents designs to derail you! That is why in your mind's eye your small flaws loom larger than life. That is exactly the accuser's plan, isn't it? He wants *your* frailties—which have yet to be healed—to seem larger than *My* life.

Nonsense! Nothing is larger than I AM. Nothing! Furthermore, why should I want you to be consumed with self-loathing and driven by fear? Hear Me, treasured one. That is exactly what I do *not* want. What I want with all of My Being is for you to feel secure in My love.

You will never know the true fear of the Lord until you understand that mercy motivates all that I do. You will never trust Me until you know I AM trustworthy. Your heart will reverence and hold Me in deepest honor *only* when you know that you can count on Me—no matter what.

I have promised to defend you, have I not? So here I AM! I know you feel helpless. Your sorrow is ever before Me. Be assured, child. Even now I AM dismantling all evil devices. Soon they will unravel before your very eyes, and you and I will laugh and sing together as they do! Consider the song of My psalmist, David: "The words of the Lord are flawless, like silver refined in a furnace seven times."

David is right. My promises are imperishable! They are as solid as eternity. They are as secure as I AM. Do you understand what that means? It means, what I say goes! No force in creation can stop it, for it is My Word that sustains the worlds. And My Word sustains you, even now. You can count on it.

Always,

Your Dad

Dearest Dreamer,

When you were younger you loved astronomy. You were a devoted stargazer. Yes, how well I recall. We have much in common, you and I. Stargazing happens to be one of My own favorite pastimes. Do you still thrill as you remember those supernovas that are exploding in multi-colored splendor? I know how you have yearned for a closer view of those pulsating quasars I posted to blink on the far away brink of infinity. And one day you shall have it.

I know also how My vast, cosmic meadows of galaxies captivate your imagination. In the daydreams of your youth you lived there more often than you lived on earth. Your loved ones were always having to call you down from the far reaches of your journeys into interstellar infinity and remind you of lunch. But even then, while others chatted and ate, your mind returned to explore the constellations.

Oh yes. I know all about you, and I AM glad you love My starry heavens. And, chosen conqueror, not only are they Mine, they are also yours. I created them all for your joy. My Word called them forth. I merely spoke, and the cosmos burst into being! It was just that simple. Hardly anyone believes it these days, but that is exactly what happened. What I say goes!

My dear child, if I can breathe a universe into existence with a mere word, why should you worry about your tomorrows? I will complete the good work I have begun in you. I AM your Father. You will and must become as I AM. Nothing ever can or ever will separate you from My love. You are Mine, and I AM yours. You ride on the strong shoulders of the Lion of Judah. I will continue to remind you of this as we approach the end of this small conflict.

Remember, this battle *is* Mine. What I say goes!

Your Omnipotent Abba

Meticulous Child,

Salvation means rescue and restoration, not reward. To achieve it yourself you must keep all the rules, all the time—and all for all the right reasons, too. Striving to be 100 percent right, every second of every minute of every hour of every day, for a lifetime—will this make you happy, let alone pleasant to live with? I hardly think so.

Yours chuckling,

Abba

# Day 210

*Psalm 27:13-14*

Restless Child,

Never fear, I AM here. I realize you are a bit wobbly at the moment. I know you find it difficult to distinguish between My voice and the thoughts of your own mind. Rest assured, My love for you is tender, and My compassion knows no limit. That is why I bless even your most faltering steps.

I know exactly where you are right now. In fact, I AM more aware of your position than you are. Even now I AM reaching out to you where you are in order to bring you to where I AM.

Will you meditate on this truth? It will greatly encourage you. The little god that religiosity often advertises gives impatiently, with grudging reluctance. That is not the God of the glad tidings of great joy, and it is not who I AM!

Holding your hand,

Dad

Searching One,

Immortality—that is your destiny, dear child. My offspring will live forever. They will outlast the constellations! I know that some people would have you believe that you can count on Me *only* if I can count on you. What nonsense! You were counting on yourself more than you trusted in My power *before* My Spirit awakened your heart to know Me.

Why would I send you a message that would catapult you back into the despair of that dark era? Legalistic minds are always setting deadlines. I AM Limitless Love, and I AM always extending lifelines.

Forever,

Dad

*Philippians 1:6*

Listening Lover,

I will not disappoint you. In your heart you have heard My Spirit whispering, "Seek the face of your Father," have you not? Then do so! Wait in My healing Presence with quiet joy. I will not hide from you. I will not shun you in anger. Holding grudges is not in My nature. I AM your constant Helper and your devoted Friend. I will never desert you. No earthly father or mother could love you as I do. You will always find acceptance with Me. And always means always!

Soon, cherished one, you will know My heart and My ways. You already walk in the path of My miraculous provision, or haven't you noticed? So be assured! I will expose every lie that any enemy utters. No harm will befall you. Not only will you savor the aroma of My Presence, you will constantly exude My fragrance. Furthermore, you will live in the *substance* of My glory and goodness.

After all, that is why I created you! That is your purpose for being.

Yours with infinite joy,

Abba

# Day 213

*Daniel 10:12-13*

Bewildered One,

Sometimes your prayers provoke satanic resistance. The ploy is to pull the plug on your hope and cause you to conclude that I have deserted you.

Nonsense! As you are waiting, what I'm really doing is increasing your inner strength and endurance. At the same time, I'm breaking through all interference and answering your prayers. I know how tired you feel, but thank you for trusting.

Your Almighty Abba

# Day 214

Weary-Hearted One,

Not everyone shares My tastes. So of course not everyone is going to like you! Many people dislike Me. Even I cannot please all people at all times. I AM Truth. I AM Reality personified. Reality *cannot* please unhappy souls as long as they prefer to live a lie. It simply is not possible. Consider yourself to be in good company, because you are!

Make it your policy to love your fellow human beings, but to practice only what I will always applaud. You already enjoy My approval and acceptance, so you can love others without fretting about whether they appreciate you or understand your heart.

Even in unfallen worlds, the finite creatures that inhabit them do not possess the ability to understand hearts as I do. I should know, shouldn't I? Are you aware that Heaven's angels even now applaud you from many realms in our house? You have done well, treasured one. Enter into joy everlasting! I AM here, so do you mind doing it now?

I led you into difficulties to show you something wonderful. You needed to learn how My love can conquer in the midst of chaos. Child, you *are* learning, I AM happy to report. When you comfort others in days to come, it will be My healing words that flow from your well-trained spirit. You will not make mere nice-sounding noises, devoid of My life and My power. Your progress delights Me!

Love always,

Dad

Cherished Child,

Searing pain exploding in every nerve cell. Agonizing thirst mingled with exhaustion. Add terror, loneliness, and the outrage of jeers and obscenities coming from His tormentors! What do you see?

Does the Crucified One reflect a God looking for reasons to reject you? I love you too much to leave you. Leaving you never occurs to My mind as an option. Conditional love does not exist in our Kingdom!

Yours tenderly,

Abba

# Day 216

Fearless Freedom Fighter,

You have been tested in the furnace of affliction. But forget the past. I AM doing a new thing. Haven't you observed it? Even now, it springs forth for our joy! You need to hear this again, so I don't mind repeating Myself. I AM your Deliverer, your Protector, your God. Above all else, I AM your loving Father. I *enjoy* teaching you. It is My delight to guide your steps.

I have promised you many times that I would enlighten you with My wisdom and shield you from harm, have I not? So forsake frenzy, child of My heart. Choose to rest in My love and enter into joy. You can count on Me. I will instruct you. When you need it, the "light" will come on inside you, and you *will* know the way you should go.

Why do I not inform you in advance of the details of situations you are facing? The reason is quite simple. If I did, your weary mind would only have more words to misconstrue. As you've already discovered, the situations themselves are always far easier than the thoughts you entertain about them beforehand. Besides, you have yearned for simplicity, haven't you? So I AM fulfilling your heart's desires. Savor sleep and relish rest, valiant warrior. I AM your Source of Security. You need nothing else. We both know that.

With all My Love,
Your Almighty Abba

Anguished Child,

Cherished one, why do you plead for My mercy? You have it. Harboring anger against self only stifles faith and fosters more failure. My children live by faith, not self-flagellation!

Ease up, little one. If only you knew My tender heart toward you. It wasn't your fault. Sorrow, confusion, and fear blinded you. Apology accepted.

I love you,

Dad

Diligent Disciple,

Again, just to say thank you for loving people more than you cherish perfection. I understand the challenge. Receive My refreshment. It's okay to take a break sometimes.

I just want to say how I appreciate your not giving up. I AM looking for faithfulness, not flawlessness.

Yours proudly,

Dad

Dear Child,

Ingratitude—yes, it hurts and I'm so sorry you've experienced it. I just want you to know that I understand, and I care. All I ask is that you not let imperfect people poison your heart with bitterness. Why let the enemy celebrate how he succeeded in stealing your song?

A satanic lie caused ingratitude to fill the hearts of Adam and Eve. As a result, My true glory became distorted in their thinking, as well as in the minds of all their offspring—but you already know the rest of the story. Even so, are you aware that My Son, Jesus Christ, is working a plan? Absolutely! He plans to *refill* with jubilant song all the sons and daughters of Adam and Eve.

One day every knee shall bow in deepest adoration, and every tongue will acclaim Christ and *give joyful thanks* for His Lordship! A lie brought the curse of ingratitude and destruction. The Living Truth—even now—by the power of His cross, is at work to reverse that satanic curse, so that thanksgiving resounds as the cosmic theme once again!

I want to thank you for pioneering to reestablish grateful song in the earth! You are a pacesetter, a kind of "firstfruits" in My plan for My cherished creation, dear child. And we both know that Heaven's reign has to begin *somewhere,* don't you agree? I so appreciate your allowing it to begin in you.

Yours with deepest sincerity,

Abba

Bewildered Liberator,

Yes, I open some doors leading into paths you would avoid if you knew about them in advance. Often your enrichment depends on your investment in others.

Trust Me! Do you have any other choice? Sometimes I let you muddle into messes to show you miracles. I AM saving you from stagnation and liberating you from boredom. Exciting, isn't it?

Love,

Dad

Psalm 145:3-16;
Galatians 5:6

Searching Child,

Today I have dropped in to remind you that you can perceive Heaven governing in all things. Yes, even at this moment I make all things new. You can see that, if you will view everything through My eyes. And you will see through My eyes if you want to, child. Only say yes, and you shall behold and enjoy!

Then you no longer will struggle and strive to produce faith, for faith does not come from parroting positive platitudes. Assurance of My love—that is what fosters faith. Faith functions by love. You have thought much about Me, and I appreciate that. But now, will you commune with Me heart to heart? I long to hold you.

Yours truly,

Abba

Learning Liberator,

Yes, I agree. Knowledge is power. Therefore, you possess power—unlimited power! Your knowledge of Me (not about Me, but of Me) grants you the wealth of infinite wisdom and might. You are not a victim. Your natural liabilities are My opportunities. Stop worrying!

Those who shy away from My power are like young eagles that shy away from soaring. They have yet to understand their identities and destinies. I put thorns in the nest to nudge them out into discovery. Exciting, isn't it?

Yours chuckling,

Dad

Troubled Child,

You have prayed for My will to be done on earth just as it is in Heaven. Have you forgotten? I haven't. When you ask for anything that harmonizes with My heart's aspirations, you can rest assured that I hear you and freely give you what you want.

As I have told you, My thoughts are not your thoughts. Your ways cannot begin to compare with the wisdom of Mine. As the heavens reach above the earth into infinity, so My ways are higher than yours. My reasoning astounds the most astute of human minds. Aren't you glad? You should be! My wisdom has saved you from many a snare, treasured one.

I will not disappoint you. Even now My Spirit is working amidst the seeming contradictions in your life, causing them to conform to My loving purpose. At the same time, you are learning to rely on My power. It is easy to tell others that you serve a God of miracles, isn't it? However, sooner or later events will arise that demand that you show people what you have been telling them. My Spirit is preparing you now for such adventures.

Do you really think I have led you this far to toss you on the scrap heap? Cease fretting! I saw your struggles long before I flung the galaxies from My fingers. Your mistakes are already accounted for, child. I AM weaving My grand design for your destiny around them. Believe in your anointing. I do!

Loving you always,
Dad

P.S. I keep all you commit to My care. I make all things beautiful in My time. All means all.

Tender-Hearted One,

A bath in sulfuric acid or an atmosphere bristling with toxic criticism—which is worse? Subtle put-downs popping out, masquerading as jokes—I never find them funny. Do you? I love showering joy and encouragement.

Those giving you a hard time are mad at Me, not you. Respond with tact. Be patient. I will soon render you unavailable. Relieved?

Blessed are the encouragers!

Your Rock of Refuge always,

Abba

Lovable Liberator,

No sane, normal father would demand that his child do the impossible. So when I tell you to be holy I'm not demanding that you instantly perfect yourself. Far less do I desire that "thou shouldest speak" and appear as though you somehow had managed to time travel from the 1500s into today's world.

Somber souls who make it a point to wear old-fashioned clothes and to strut about scowling at other people have missed My point completely. Holiness is not weirdness! It is a pity that some folks have muddled sanctification and sanctimony together as synonymous terms. Don't you agree?

When I call you to holiness, I AM inviting you into wholeness, the wholeness that emerges from our friendship—from our walking and talking together. I also yearn to empower you so that hurting people will find healing as you touch them. I long that you and I intoxicate everyone everywhere with the wine of Real Love—Authentic Love—so they become irreversibly addicted.

You want the same thing, child. I know that. But as you have already observed, power minus purity equals corruption and clearly, neither of us wants that for you

Furthermore, I yearn for your happiness. Do you realize that unless you are maturing so that you increasingly reflect My true glory, you will never be happy? Believe Me! I know what it takes to make you happy, for I AM the Happy God. Therefore, you "shall" be happy because I AM. That is My commitment to you. Are you surprised? I don't mind telling again: I have no interest whatsoever in religiosity! I AM interested in you. Thanks for taking time for us.

Yours with joyful anticipation,
Abba

Treasured Child,

Peace—what is it? Peace is what happens when you learn to rest in the truth that I AM All-Loving and All-Powerful!

My Son has given you peace that the world can neither offer nor steal. Don't allow anyone to talk you out of it. Your feelings fluctuate, but My love never fails. Never, never, not ever!

Yours with all power,

Dad

Inquiring Child,

Why do you look to books or to other human beings for guidance? You are wrong to imagine that I prefer the company of My other children over yours. Shhh! Listen, cherished one. To your ears I may be speaking softly, but I AM speaking. I AM not distanced from you by light-years of cosmic infinity; I dwell inside you. I enjoy you! Nothing pleases Me more than to be your Friend and constantly make Myself available to you.

The more your heart becomes convinced that I love you, the less you will worry about straying from My will. Committed friends tend to share the same interests, the same high aspirations. As a result, their hearts lead them toward the same goals. How much more is this true where you and I are concerned. Our love-bond makes you heir to unlimited power!

So, child, why waste these moments of waiting with worry? Abraham fathered Ishmael in an attempt to hasten My plan of giving him a son. Do you recall? Even so, in due time, I gave him Isaac, the son of My promise. Centuries later I sent My angel Gabriel to inform aged Zechariah that his elderly wife, Elizabeth, would bear him a son. He balked in unbelief when he first heard of My radical plan. So, for a season he lost the use of his tongue. However, little John the Baptist was born. Years later he became the world's greatest prophet and paved the way for the coming Messiah.

Consider! Abraham blundered ahead of My plan while Zechariah lagged behind. Nevertheless, I fulfilled My word to them both, did I not? So it will be with you, chosen conqueror! Be at peace concerning My process and your part in it. I AM! Should you need any adjustment, I will tell you, never fear. In fact, not only will I tell you, I also will help you! Haven't I always?

Thank you for trusting,

Your Devoted Dad

Generous Child,

This will not be the last time your tender heart causes you to empty your pockets. Isn't living by faith stimulating?

Reckon it as a gift offered to Me, and you will no longer feel robbed or plundered. What is given to Me remains with Me. Have you forgotten we are family?

Proudly your Provider,

Dad

Hurting One,

Yes, I have called you to follow Christ as He continues to pour out His life in self-giving love. Even so, I have not called you to become a doormat under the grinding heels of the ruthless. Offering your life to Me moment by moment as a loving sacrifice is one thing. Submitting to sadism is a different matter entirely!

Did David allow demented Saul to impale him with a spear, or did he dodge it? In Nazareth, did Jesus submit to a crazed mob and allow them to hurl Him from a cliff? Read for yourself: "He walked right through the crowd and went on His way."

How did He manage that feat? Your Lord submitted to Me. He did not submit to murderers. So just as I had once parted the Red Sea, My finger carved a path through the crowd that sought to destroy Him. I delivered My dear Son from His enemies! Thus your Good Shepherd was able to say, "No one takes My life. I lay it down when I choose."

Child, you can trust Me to grant you the same power. It breaks My heart when My unwitting children submit to self-appointed spiritual guides who abuse them. Why do they submit? They do so simply because their abusers have brainwashed them to believe that I require it! Wives endure violence and children suffer untold agony—all because confused people have taught them that My holiness demands it.

Not so! If that were true, I would not have rescued My people Israel from their cruel captors in Egypt. Nor would I have instructed the mother of baby Moses to hide him from Pharaoh, who had issued a death warrant against him.

Please hear Me, hurting one. I AM a God of mercy. When will all of My children believe this? Cling to Me. As I have told you, making ways where there are none is My specialty.

Yours with deepest compassion,

Abba

Tender One,

I have seen your tears and heard your cries. I've walked with you through sorrows that only you and I have known. And satan tells you I plan humiliation and grief for you? Don't believe a word of it!

Tenderly,

Abba

*Matthew 12:18-21*

Bewildered Child,

   I will never desert you. It is not in My nature to abandon hurting people. My love-covenant is not based on your success or performance; it is founded on My unfailing mercy.

   "What on earth is happening?" you have asked. I'm training
you to trust. That is what is happening. I know that you face
many obstacles in your journey toward wholeness, and you are
right. I have not removed some of your more disreputable-looking flaws by a sovereign act of My power. If I had, you would have
become blind to your need for My tender mercy. You would have
imagined that you somehow had managed to earn My love. By
confusing the world's idea of respectability for "godliness," you
would have settled for far less than My best.

   I AM not in the business of reproducing replicas of the world's
stereotypical success images. Far less am I interested in manu-
facturing religious robots. The world is overrun by too many of
them already! Don't you agree? I have no use for such facsimiles,
as well-rounded and nice as they may appear to be. I'm forming
a reigning family of co-deliverers who are radiant with My glory.
This company of compassionate restorers will reflect the True
Light of My Son Jesus Christ, and liberate the world with My
transforming love.

   Thanks for listening and for your patience.

                                                      I love you!

                                                      Dad

Worried Child,

Things were possessing you. That is why I took them away—not permanently, but just for a season. I AM making use of these days to remove all impurities in your deepest self that have brought you pain. These toxic elements are the result of your confusing satanic lies for the truth. But never fear! All will be well. The feelings of paranoia you are experiencing are normal. They are not your fault. They usually accompany withdrawal. Interestingly, you will find yourself more at peace from this point on. I know how your personality functions!

Never fear, chosen one. My Son will not fail or become discouraged. Your Strong Deliverer will labor on until He has established full deliverance in that awesome, if tiny, bit of earth called "you." I have destined you to become like Him! Because your Elder Brother and I have borne patiently with your frailties, compassion will crown your ministry.

Cherished one, when you know what is happening, it is easier to be happy, isn't it? It is not impossible to be happy when you are not "in the know," but that is a lesson you will enjoy later on. For now, pursue love, laughter—and life. The whole reason I disentangled you from all of that exhausting paraphernalia was to free you to breathe and to enjoy life—Real Life! Only in the midst of Life's enjoyment can you discover the "real you." You've spent enough time struggling to be a facsimile, a silly hodgepodge of "everyone else's" ideas.

Consider yourself rescued! You are. You are Mine and deeply loved. Thank you for trusting!

Your Mighty Fortress,
Abba

Strong Conqueror,

 The more you learn to live with Me in the present, the more foreign the memories of old pursuits will appear when they crop up on occasion. This is why I keep "harping" about the perils of self-scrutiny unsanctioned by Me.

Love,

Dad

Daring Explorer,

Surprise! Here I AM again, assuring you that I AM greater than your keen intellect. I have all kinds of interesting ways of cropping up, don't I?

What! Me give up on the Church? You must be joking. As for organized religiosity, as you well know, that is something I have never endorsed! So how could I give up on something I never had anything to do with in the first place? I have no intention of ever giving up on the world, so there is no way I will ever give up on the Church. That is because, in its purest essence, the Church is made up of radical rescuers like you. Such individuals detest religious hypocrisy while they yearn to lavish healing love on marginalized and suffering people.

The Church—the true Body of Christ—is dedicated to bringing deliverance to the lost and displaced of the world. Organized religion, for the most part, aspires to escape the world and "go to Heaven." My anointed world-deliverers yearn to bring Heaven to earth. And they pray that My purpose will be fully done on earth, just as it is in Heaven.

Delighted to answer your prayers, as ever! You didn't think I heard them, did you? Ha!

Abba

Loving Child,

Are you aware that I love agnostics and atheists? Many of these are "good Samaritans" and are among the most honest people I know. They are not afraid to ask hard questions. They refuse to pretend reverence toward abuse that parades itself as "spirituality." Many who question My existence come through with flying colors when it comes down to what is dear to My heart: *actually helping people.* You and I are better friends than you know!

I was just thinking of Jesus. How much honest investigating have you done regarding His claims? I couldn't resist asking. By the way, I interpret all heart longings as prayers. So be prepared for a few notable miracles. I know how desperately you need them.

With deepest understanding,

Your Real Dad

Weary Child,

   Just a review of the obvious. Don't demand respect and you will receive it. Demand it, and you will become the target of jokes and contempt. Just be you. Do you mind? I like you. Yes, I realize I'm repeating Myself, and be advised! This won't be the last time!

Loving you always,

Dad

Inquiring Restorer,

I don't mind repeating Myself. So again, holiness means wholeness. It is wholeness, resplendent with the radiance of My glory and heart-purity. How deeply I desire that for you! Why? I think you deserve it. I created you in My image and called you good, long before you awakened to life in this world.

I AM called Good. Therefore, holiness is your heritage, your destiny. Without it, no person ever can or ever will see Me. Those who are not whole lack the clarity of vision to perceive and appreciate love. And, of course. Love—Unfailing Pure Love—is who I AM. That is why you must beware of bitterness or chronic self-pity, child of My heart.

Always Your Healer, I AM!

Dad

Searching Child,

Which is more important—what people have done to you and for you? Or what Christ has done for you and in you? Only ask, and I will open your eyes to see! You are not wrong to want everyone to love and understand you. The day will come when they will.

For now, though, you must bear in mind that even the most spiritually sensitive human beings see as "through a glass, darkly." So your priority must be receiving My love and giving it away. If you make it your priority to influence other people to understand and love you, you will only break your own heart.

We both think it is right that everyone should love everyone. Yet for that to happen it has to begin with someone. Can you think of anyone?

I AM so blessed having you in My life!

Your Devoted Abba

Inquiring Truth Seeker,

Spiritual authority. What is it? It is simply the natural quality of leadership that emerges from years of walking with Me. True spiritual authority doesn't need the officious-looking trappings of worldly authority. Relax! I have called you to lead others now because I trust the teachable heart I have formed in you.

Without a doubt!

Your Devoted Dad

*Philippians 3:12*

Treasured One,

You gave what you had. So will you please stop nit-picking with your past? After you gave what you had, I gave what I had. So I more than made up for your lack.

Since then I have expanded your reserves. You now enjoy greater riches, and you will possess even more to give in days to come. However, when increased abundance arrives, you mustn't look back and criticize what you gave today by comparing it to what you acquired later on. Such negative analysis only wounds your heart and causes My gentle Spirit to grieve for you. My Spirit longs to encourage you, child. Keeping you running scared and glancing back over your shoulder is *not* Heaven's agenda!

You will be far happier once the truth comes home to your heart that My sufficiency and your seeming insufficiency are separate subjects entirely. Is it any wonder that you have felt spread so thin? Your trying to be "God" (the Everlasting Fountain of Supply) for everyone else is the culprit. Repent!

Yours grinning,

Dad

Trusted Restorer,

Do you enjoy paying hard-earned money only to receive half-hearted service? Shoddy workmanship? Then, before you start squawking about fair pay, make sure you're actually doing the job. And don't forget My extra mile policy. Thanks!

Loving you always,

Abba

Valiant Conqueror,

Knowing—possessing knowledge that is deep, settled, and unshakable—is better than having a feeling. Feelings are sporadic and fleeting. Feelings can fool you and lead you astray. But faith that springs from the *solid certainty* that I love you will propel you into astonishing feats of power!

Such faith has nothing to do with feelings. Child, you are too old to scrutinize your emotions and look for odd sensations. I have crowned you with My wisdom! You have the mind of Christ. Your anointing shatters prison doors and heals broken hearts! Walk in it. Trust in it. My Spirit will not disappoint you.

You learned this truth long ago, but lately I have been helping you to review it again. Why? You already know why, but I don't mind telling you what you already know. Promotion demands preparation. I AM promoting you to perform new exploits of power, just as I promised you earlier. So I have chosen first to show you the strength of the faith foundation that I have established inside you. That discovery will empower you to launch out, laughing in the face of fear! Now go. Go with the confidence of a conqueror! You might as well, treasured one, because that is what you are!

With deepest confidence,

Your Dad

Beloved Searcher,

Do you really think you'd find it easier to exercise faith if I kept bombarding you with miracles? Why didn't My multiplied miracles cause faith to flourish in the multitudes who followed Moses in the wilderness? Ingratitude devours trust. What a monster!

Helpfully,

Abba

Dear Child,

The words I speak are breath and life! Why should I harass you with sudden rebukes and addle you with surprise assignments spoken through someone else? You constantly make yourself available to Me. Am I unable to address you personally? Any "message from God" that ignores our previous discussions and responds to your penitent tears with pompous threats is a hoax.

Some of My less-seasoned prophets have yet to learn the difference between their opinions and Mine. When My Spirit enlightens them to see a thing, they assume that, having seen it, they understand it. They confuse knowledge for wisdom. At other times, a man who seeks to convey My word to another fails to understand that I intended that message for *him*. Even so, child, I encourage you not to become cynical about prophecy. Simply test all things and hold fast to that which is good. And please, stay in touch with the good sense of humor I have given you! Ninety percent of spiritual discernment resides within that gift.

Thank you for listening,

Dad

Deep Thinker,

You are right. Like a loose bolt banging around in the works, so the Man, Jesus, clatters in the machinery of materialistic philosophy. Why do you think I sent Him? A well-documented resurrection has a way of unraveling secular skepticism. Interesting, isn't it, how you opened up to this page today...

You'll be hearing from Me again!

Dad

# Day 246

Searching Child,

I AM Love, and Love never fails. That means Love never gives up—not ever. That also means you are in for an exhausting trip when you try to bail out and do your own thing, or haven't you noticed?

Welcome back! The reason you bailed out was because you imagined that your Good Shepherd and I wanted to be happy at your expense. As you recall, that is the same silly lie the serpent told Adam and Eve.

"God wants to keep *you* groveling in stupidity while He enjoys all the benefits of boundless knowledge!" satan whined.

However, you already know how the story goes after that, don't you?

With you always,

Abba

Treasured Child,

Today I want to reaffirm our friendship and remind you of My commitment to you. Your Lord said, "If anyone loves Me, he will keep My word." So do you know what I AM committed to do? I AM committed to cause you to love Jesus Christ with a passion that boggles your mind and blessedly breaks your heart.

Never fear, I AM not planning any disasters for you. I plan to do what I have always been doing. I will continue ordering your circumstances so that you keep coming nose-to-nose with your loving Savior. What do you think of the recent rescues your Lord and I engineered on your behalf? Did they surprise you? Just to confirm again: any interpretation of Scripture that represents Me as being less reliable and patient than an earthly father *has* to be wrong. Period!

That does not mean that living apart from My counsel and nurture is painless. You already know that, so I need not elaborate. In My embrace you will find healing. Let's enjoy being together.

All things new—that is My promise to My creation, treasured child, and it is My promise to you. Behold! I make *all* things new.

With unfailing power and devotion,

Abba

# Day 248

Frantic Scrambler,

   Make friends with your mortality, and you will transcend it. Embrace your limitations as allies, and you will forget them. Peace arrives only when warring ceases. You possess wisdom and life everlasting! Why battle for what is already yours?

Forever through Jesus,

Abba

Treasured Restorer,

Yes, I know that people offer you only shoddy performance while they demand that which is most costly from you. Sadly, too many who claim to follow Christ are among the most notorious perpetuators of that injustice. They want *your* best gifts and efforts, yet they habitually look for ways to give you as little as possible.

But, child, you no longer labor under the tyranny of tit-for-tat legalism. You now realize that My love secures you and that you need nothing else. So I want to thank you for making every effort to live in the Light of My Son, your Good Shepherd. I AM trusting you to continue following Him as He pours out His life for self-serving people who are not easy to love.

These days you no longer strive in frenzy, fearing My hopeless abandonment. Such irrational religiosity no longer warps your perception of who I AM and how I treat My little neighbors. Hope and holy desire now spur you on to perform daring deeds of deliverance! My smallest wish is your command, because you have grown to cherish and trust Me for who I AM.

Good! That is the heart submission I have yearned to see happen in you. Now you are free to love—truly love. So at this point we can get on with your life. Our life! Irreversible victories await us.

Now, about those prayers...I have not been ignoring them, cherished one. Will you believe Me? As you well know, I can produce immediate results, but I refuse to specialize in them. If I did, neither you nor I nor anyone else would appreciate the results of all of those lovely looking, instant "solutions."

Think about it. And while you are thinking, consider some of those forty-five-year-old spoiled brats you've had to put up with in your lifetime. Such people were nurtured in an environment where nearly all their demands were met immediately! Has getting what they wanted the moment they piped up for it turned them into happy people? You and I both know the answer to that. Do you enjoy their company? No? Neither do I. Nor does anyone else!

Thank you for trusting.

Yours with devotion,

Dad

*Psalm 16:11*

Diligent Disciple,

I love laughter. You can often find Me rollicking in the midst of it. But like you, I cannot laugh at the pain of hurting people, or celebrate the disgrace or weakness of others. Thank you, thank you for your compassion-driven fury against such abuse and injustice.

Proudly,

Your Dad

Dear Servant-Hearted Child,

Brilliant! At last you are seeing the light. The secret to overcoming fear of people's opinions is to love them too much to care how they may feel about you. Do you now see why I have been keeping you so busy? These days you find it nearly impossible to focus on your inadequacies or on those of others.

I AM overjoyed by your progress! In getting out of yourself you are discovering My True Self and finding your true self as well. Thus you are learning to live a life of love. Personally, I can't think of a better way to live, can you?

With admiration,

Abba

Faithful Child,

I want to thank you for bearing patiently with My leaders. One reason I brought you into their lives was to show them the power of unconditional love. One reason I brought them into your life was so that you may profit by learning from their mistakes. Aren't you glad I love and trust you so much?

Child, I have promised that you shall have no other gods before Me. As you have noticed, I AM fulfilling that promise! I keep giving you glimpses of the chinks in the armor of My servants—who also happen to be your would-be idols. I know that you understand why I do so. It is not to enable you to discourage or destroy them. Rather, I show you their frailties because I AM trusting you to cover and shield them with your love and your prayers. As you and I both know very well, it is love—not criticism and scorn—that covers a multitude of sins. What a blessing you are!

Yours with highest esteem,

Abba

Inquiring Seeker,

No, I AM not losing patience. I've spoken words of life to your heart again and again. And I will continue to do so! But, sooner or later you must respond to My words. Those who hear them can enjoy their benefit only if they heed them.

Always your friend,

Abba

Despondent Child,

Self-pity is a sinister spirit, a tiny demon that speaks loudly of "justice." That wily spirit's ploy is to fill your heart with resentment, grief, and rage. Why? Just to keep you miserable! That is why.

Have you forgotten? Self-pity always seduces its victim with the reasonable-sounding snares of respect, appreciation, and fairness.

Then it whispers, "Are you receiving *your* dues?"

The last response that little devil wants to hear from you is, "Perhaps not! But did Jesus receive His?"

At all costs he must keep that line of reasoning from surfacing! It would utterly spoil his devious scheme to keep you shackled to the idolatry of human opinion.

I know you are tired of that exhausting syndrome. Self-pity never brought you any joy, did it? It even failed to deliver its promised reward of "self-respect."

You have let other people declare your value. You have forgotten that in My sight you possess infinite value. Repent! Resume praying for an outpouring of My Spirit upon those whom I have called you to serve, and just keep being the blessing you are. Many thanks, and God be with you!

But of course, I AM!

Dad

Dear Child,

How do My mature children evaluate success? They define success as "sanctified stubbornness"! They freely admit their frailty while refusing to allow past failures to haunt them. Their dreams drive them on toward their destinies. I think you're growing up!

Yours proudly,

Abba

Treasured Child,

You need not try to convince Me. I know you cannot heal yourself. Your own efforts have failed because I alone can do this work. You are powerless within yourself, hurting one, and I don't expect you to perform the impossible! I only ask that you do one thing: abide in My loving nurture.

If at times you find yourself unable to do that, just remember—I AM committed to you anyway. I will remove all obstacles and gently maneuver you into My healing Presence. Isn't that how I drew you to Myself in the first place? Yes, and even now I AM doing it. You have not chosen Me. I have chosen you; you are worth *all* My efforts.

I know your heart. I understand your frailty. I know your deepest desires and take into account every factor that contributes to your pain. I know you did not "choose" these factors. I know that many of them were already present when you arrived in this world. You certainly did not choose to be born!

No, you were *My* idea. That is why you are here! So will you rest in My tender care and stop reasoning? Will you turn your gaze from the past and walk on? You cannot successfully move forward and look backward at the same time. Turn around, child! Follow Me! Have you forgotten? That is what "repentance" means.

Yours with everlasting commitment,

Dad

Shaken Conqueror,

It's not too late to start again. Savor My friendship and refuse to look back. Refuse to let appearances erode your resolve or plunder your peace. This time you will go in My power. Ha! Do you realize our enemies are already scrambling for cover?

Yours with renewed mercies,

Abba

*Psalm 34:4-5;*
*Galatians 5:16;*
*Philippians 3:10-15*

Sorrowful One,

I AM not your enemy. I love you, and I AM on your side. Nothing has changed between us. So please, child, stop degrading yourself, will you? Human wrath cannot foster a climate where virtue can grow and flourish. Harboring anger toward self spawns only frustration, despair, and more failure.

Surely you have noticed by now that self-hatred fuels lust. Why? It destroys hope. That is why. In the absence of hope, irresponsible behavior erupts and mind-binding addictions begin to tyrannize and destroy. That is because despair's child is insanity; it can give birth to no other offspring.

Yes, godly sorrow does lead to repentance. I could not agree more. After all, My Spirit authored those words. However, there is nothing godly about groveling in self-loathing and remorse! That is not at all what I have in mind for you; My heart yearns for something far better.

Hurting one, let us embrace. I long to hold you close and to flood your aching heart with joy. Remember! My wrath lasts but for a moment. So child, why do you extend your anger beyond the boundaries of Mine? All victories and all virtues spring from our fellowship, not from your fury or frenzy. That is what Paul meant when he said that when you walk in the Spirit, you will not fulfill the desires of the flesh. The more you learn how to love (and I AM here to teach you), the less you will desire anything that is contrary to My highest aspirations for you.

Thank you for listening,

Abba

# Day 259

*Ephesians 2:8-10;*
*Colossians 2:9*

Fretful Child,

Stop reviewing your track record and choose to review Mine. You can never score high enough to earn My favor and blessings. They are already yours! As I have told you, it is not your manipulation but My mercy that moves mountains. Just to adjust your thinking.

Lovingly,

Abba

Lonely Liberator,

Thank you for trusting Me—come what may and no matter what. I just want to confirm that yes, I allowed you to endure treachery at the hands of My wayward children. I trusted you in that trial. It was not to punish you, but to train you to recognize what ministry is not—and what love is not.

Now you know how *not* to treat hurting people I entrust into your care. And of course, knowing how you must not deal with them, you see all the more clearly how you must nurture and love them.

Will you please trust Me with your reputation? Rest assured, the coming flood tide of My favor on you will astonish everyone, including your detractors! They will be shocked into silence, and I will break their hard hearts. One by one, they will come to you seeking forgiveness. Do you doubt My ability to arrange such events? You shouldn't! I have vindicated you before.

I've also brought you down a few notches on occasions, have I not? (I always enjoy seeing you smile!) Oh yes, I know how to vindicate the humble and bring low the lofty. As you well know, to the pure I show Myself pure and to the crafty and self-serving I show Myself shrewd. I know how to deal with all kinds of people, cherished one. Now will you trust Me? The time will come when those who hurt you will love and treasure you as I do. Meanwhile, I AM shutting the mouths of "the lions."

Rest! Sleep, wounded warrior. Allow Me to fight your battles. You will like the outcome. I promise!

Forever your Strong Fortress,

Abba

Trusted Deliverer,

Why take personal offense when strangers fail to treat you with courtesy? If they saw you as a person, they would love you as I do. The love-starved inhabiting our world suffer impaired vision, perceiving only human-shaped shadows.

Thanks for understanding,

Dad

Committed Conqueror,

I know it is difficult, but please continue to sow the seeds of mercy. I want you to reap their harvest. Refuse to jump to conclusions based on what your physical eyes see or what your natural ears hear. Resolve to allow My Spirit to teach you, and judge nothing before the appointed time. That includes judging yourself, treasured one.

I have placed you in a position of honor, a position of trust. I have chosen you to bear the burdens of those who are weak. You know why, don't you? I do. I know the strength I have deposited in your life. So I have placed you where you are, to love the lowly, and yes, even the unlovely. I know you remember how I loved you into wholeness when you were despair-ridden and broken. I dealt tenderly with your frailties, did I not? Yes, I was merciful even when you were ill-tempered, cynical, and faithless.

Child, I was patient with you as your healing progressed. I do not require that you compromise the truth. All I ask is that you continue to *live* in truth, and follow My example and do for others as I have done for you. Then you will speak the truth in love, as My Spirit enlightens the eyes of your heart to see as I do.

Yours with deepest trust,

Dad

Devoted Child,

Again! Focusing on self only multiplies misery. Rest securely in My limitless mercy. Return to joy! Thus, you'll remain on My miracle-packed path of provision. It's impossible to nose-dive into clouds of doubt and despair and, at the same time, soar in the jet stream of faith.

Yours, joyfully,

Dad

Cherished but Angry One,

You can hate your way out of your inheritance, but you cannot hate your way out of My love. It just cannot happen. My love led you into My arms, and it will lead you back into them again. It is only a matter of time.

I gladly share My Kingdom with you, but you cannot reign in our Kingdom of light as long as you allow the tyranny of darkness to reign over you. Resentment is gross darkness! It will never establish the glad government of Heaven's True Light in a chaotic world wracked with pain.

This warning has nothing to do with My depriving you of your reigning position, treasured one. It has everything to do with *your* abdicating your throne and allowing bitterness to ascend and take charge. That is the simple truth.

I care about your pain, and I love you with all of My heart. I cry with you. Will you draw near and allow Me to hold you? This burden is too heavy for you.

Your Strong Refuge always,

Abba

# Day 265

My Dear Child,

Nothing! Do you hear Me? Nothing in all creation ever will or ever can separate us. Nothing! That doesn't mean we won't have to sort through sundry problems on occasion. But I think you're worth it. In fact, I can't imagine life without you. You are a blessing!

Truly!

Abba

Sorrowful One,

Why do you cry? I have shown you how Kingdom policy requires that eternal gains often first appear as losses. Don't despair. You will only have to return to hope if you do. Consider Christ! He defeated death, but He conquered by yielding, not by resisting.

When the world's Savior, beaten and bleeding, hung in agony on His cross, no one could foresee His victory. His loved ones could feel only horror and stifled outrage for His humiliation and pain. When they gazed upon their mutilated Friend, they could see only disaster, injustice, the gross wickedness of corrupt human government, dying dreams.

But were they right? Did they see the whole picture? You know the answer to that. Tearful child, always remember: Christ's cross portrays perfectly the way of My wisdom, for it shows that in Heaven's economy life *must* prevail over death, even if death may at first appear to have the upper hand.

So when My wisdom is at work, things usually appear worse before they look better. It was the same with Abraham and Sarah as they awaited the birth of their son, Isaac, was it not? It was. They died to their dream of bearing a son. Years later, Isaac's son Jacob was tricked into marrying Leah and forced to postpone his marriage to Rachel for yet another seven years. Jacob's favorite son, Joseph, tasted a similar and perhaps a deeper sorrow. His dream bit the dust when his own brothers sold him into slavery.

Do you think young Joseph thought his imprisonment in Egypt even faintly resembled a promotion? Hardly! I heard him quietly sobbing himself to sleep many nights, so I should know. Yet Joseph rose to be second in command over all Egypt. He became the king's most trusted counselor and the deliverer of multitudes of people. Joseph also became the hero of his family, including his brothers who had abused and betrayed him.

I AM the God of Abraham, Isaac, and Jacob; and as with Joseph, I still turn imprisonments into promotions. I haven't lost My touch! Your own life fully demonstrates this fact. I know your pain. Again, your dreams are suffering violence, treasured one. But in the roar of that violence you can hear the low rumble of resurrection power resurging—if you will become quiet and listen.

Tenderly,

Dad

Diligent Disciple,

If My children name it and claim it loud and long enough, I just may let them have it. Don't you remember how the children of Israel received King Saul for their efforts? Please, child. Let's enjoy relationship!

Have you noticed that as you have grown older you have found yourself longing more and more for simplicity?

I want you to have that. It will make life more worthwhile for you—to say nothing of making you more fun to live with!

Yours with a grin,

Dad

Hesitant Conqueror,

It's like skydiving. Leaping out of an airplane from 10,000 feet above the earth is not easy—but it is fun! And that's putting it mildly. *Exhilarating* is a better word, as any seasoned skydiver will tell you.

Selling all you have, or better yet, giving it all away to follow Christ is like skydiving. The same is true when it comes to heeding My gentle heart-whisper and daring to step out (seemingly into nowhere!) in obedience.

Do you know why some people become sullen, critical, negative, hard to get along with? They are bored! That is why. I built them for adventure, not boredom, and their spirits are restless to soar. Can you relate?

I know that some of your loved ones and fellow workers have trouble understanding you. Even so, I like you, even in your grumpy moods! I know that you will obey Me sooner or later. I know you better than you know yourself!

Yours with all power, always!

Abba

Trembling Child,

Don't hesitate to smile and own up to your past, when questioned. If need be, shock the self-righteous! Someone must impart hope and save searching people. Will you do it? Your reputation rests in good hands. Mine!

I don't mind looking ridiculous to redeem foolish people. If at times I must appear weak in the sight of the world, so be it! My policy is to submit to crucifixion while staging a resurrection that will astound doubting minds and heal hurting hearts. Make friends with My policies, and refuse to worry about tomorrow. Enjoy exploits!

Yours with delight,

Dad

# Day 270

Worried Child,

You know that I love you too much to say yes to all your requests, don't you? However! The law of sowing and reaping is working for you, not against you. Which do you suppose packs the most power? The seeds of love and faith or the seeds of doubt and failure? Think about it.

With joyful expectancy,

Abba

Trusted Liberator,

You have yet to obey Me fully in this, so I will keep reminding you—cease fretting about yourself! Cease worrying about My battles. They are Mine, are they not? Believe in your anointing. I do! I have always trusted My Holy Spirit. You *are* making progress. These days it is becoming harder for you to wallow in the mire of doubt. I have noticed that, and I know that you have noticed it too. You are beginning to enjoy living in trust.

Good! That is because of our "at-one-ment." You live in Christ and He lives in Me. Is there a more secure place where you could be? I hardly think so. In time, not only will you think as I think, you also will feel as I feel. You will know *with deepest assurance* that I love you and that you are Mine.

What has made it so difficult for you to live in trust? I will tell you. Beneath the surface of back-breaking self-effort lurks the suspicion that evil packs more power than good. That suspicion is what fuels the paranoia that empowers all legalistic systems, too many of which advertise themselves as proclaimers of Christ. Amazing, isn't it? But it is true. Many of My unwitting children struggle, and strain to achieve victory, yet they live in despair and pain. It has yet to dawn on them that through Christ's triumph over death I have granted them victory. I have abolished sin once and for all!

So I don't see sin when I look at you. I see the new creation your Savior has made you to be. Your life isn't about perfecting self. It's about knowing Me. It's just that simple.

Victoriously,
Your Dad

Rushing Warrior,

What is good? Why is it stronger than evil? In your Lord's opinion there is only One who qualifies to be called Good—the very One who speaks to you now. Yes, Good happens to be who I AM. Good is not a what, but a Who! So how can any evil, however fiercely entrenched, outlast Almighty God?

Slow down, calm down, settle down. Choose to trust the Good Light who lives inside you. Decide again to rely on the still, small voice that leads you. I will not leave unfinished the work I have begun in you. I did *not* devise My own defeat when I created you, dear child. What would have been the point?

Do not allow anyone or any influence to remove you from the hope of this wonderful news I'm sharing with you! It is sheer joy having you in My life. Every day I delight to constantly present you spotless in *My* sight. So please do not deny Me that joy by struggling to appear righteous in the sight of someone else. Many thanks!

Yours with unfailing commitment,

Abba

Harassed Child,

Satan said what? Ha! Ha! Ha! Ha! Ha! Ha! Ha! Ha! Ha! Ha! Ha! Ha! Ha! Ha! Ha! Ha! Ha! Ha! Ha! Ha! Ha! Ha! Ha! Ha!

This is what you need to say to the enemy more often.

Your Abba

# Day 274

Weary One,

I delight in diversity, don't you? Our Kingdom is like a tiny seed. When it is planted, it grows into a massive tree—resilient, lush, and vibrant. Birds of every variety alight in its branches and enjoy rest and a sense of safety and belonging.

The world's kingdom despises diversity. Its tree springs from a synthetic seed, believe it or not. However, it does give birth to a tree that is large and lovely to behold, if lethal to life and variety. (This season the seed is available mainly in pastels, as I recall.) This artificial wonder spawns a tree that sprouts silicone branches of near-perfect symmetry, laden with fruit that is large and decorative—and inedible.

Many, many fowls of a banal sameness flock to its foliage. They all look alike, flap their wings alike, lay eggs alike, chirp alike, build nests alike, hop alike, and sing alike. They even go through the ritual of mating alike! Though, oddly, they seem incapable of mating for life. Even so, these creatures do exhibit remarkable qualities. For example, they can instantly vaporize into nonexistence when decreed to be "out of fashion." Then, as if on cue, they can flash into re-existence, all of them sporting *this* year's colors and plumage.

Child, I know it seems a "fowl" thing to ask, but My heart for you compels Me to pose a question. Of the two trees I have described, which do you find more inviting? I will let you sow another silicone seed and grow another look-alike tree, if that is what you want. But are you sure the world's befuddled birds will flock in great numbers to roost on its branches? Bear in mind that the branches of that tree will be identical to the ones they are already occupying elsewhere.

Here is My point: I think you are trying too hard to fit in. When will you choose to enjoy just being the delight I have made you to be? One can waste a lifetime, striving to conform to a "norm" held by a fictitious majority that simply could not care less. I love you as you are! Your uniqueness is what makes you special to Me. I mean that.

Love always,

Dad

# Day 275

Psalm 68:1-3;
Luke 10:18-20;
Romans 8:35-39

Awakening Warrior,

Tired of being victimized? Rebel against despair and dare to resume pursuing our dreams! Savor freedom! Celebrate your independence from bondage to fear. And remember! You can always count on Me, even when you cannot count on yourself. Always, always, always!

You heard Me right the first time! Go in peace. My loving wisdom saturates your spirit.

Your Dad

# Day 276

*Ephesians 4:17-32; 5;*
*Matthew 26:52;*
*Titus 2:11; Hebrews 12:29*

Distracted Child,

Thank you in advance for being kind to yourself! Feeding a fantasy only fuels lust and intensifies its gluttony so that nothing can satisfy it. Are you aware that another word for lust is *covetousness?* Covetousness spawns all kinds of misery. It unravels the rationality of all who allow it to rule. It empties bank accounts, fills hospitals and mortuaries, destroys dreams, erodes trust, and breaks hearts. And that is not all; a lust-driven life—a life ruled by covetousness—renders *authentic* relationships impossible. I know you, child. That is *not* what you want out of life.

In Christ, My grace has appeared in the world to show everyone how to say "no" to evil and how to say "yes" to Real Life—how to relish Real Life! Some people wrongly imagine that because I AM Love, that means I do not allow consequences. That is a lie, cherished one. Children who play with fire get burned. And as Jesus said, "...all they that take the sword shall perish with the sword."

Do you know what would be the most unkind thing I could do to you or to anyone else? It would be to let abuse that calls itself "love" forever have its way with our world. That definitely applies to spiritual abuse. It also applies to physical abuse of every variety. I will not—indeed, I cannot—allow evil to devour My cherished creation. It is not going to happen. I intend to make all things new! Satan's days are numbered. The tyranny of sin and death *will* come to an end. I love you. That is why I tell you the truth.

ABBA CALLING

I want us to co-labor in establishing Love's dominion world-wide! If you choose not to reign with Me and opt to establish your own kingdom instead, I will still love you with all of My heart. Furthermore, I will not be your enemy. But you need to know that you will have become *My* enemy—Love's enemy. I AM kind to My opponents, of course. That is, insofar as they will allow Me to be. However, I will *not* ensure their safety or happiness at any cost. Sooner or later all who persist in using other people to serve their own selfish agendas discover that I AM a *Consuming Fire*.

Yours with unceasing devotion,

Abba

Wandering One,

Long ago an ambitious angel started a rumor. Do you recall? He accused his Creator of being the ultimate "Killjoy." My first human children believed him. Do you believe him? I honestly don't think you do—not in your deepest heart. You know by experience that I AM your Real Source of Joy.

Please understand that it is not My intention to offend you, treasured one. My intention is to keep you on track with Reality. Your highest good is My deepest desire, and you know that. You and I both know that!

You delight me.

Abba

Searching Child,

Do you feel your liver, your pancreas, your cerebral cortex or thyroid? Why do you struggle to feel My Presence? It's time you made friends with My Personality. I enjoy quietness. Strength surges and faith flourishes in quietness.

Forever yours with confidence,

Father

Weary Restorer,

How right you are! Criticism nearly always comes at a bad time. Just when you are juggling a thousand crystal goblets and breaking your neck to do everything right—zap! Like a swift arrow shot out of the ozone, a sharp word from a faultfinder pierces your heart. "Why do you always...?" wheedles the voice. Or worse, your detractor announces, "God has given me a word for you!" Sound familiar? You forget that I hear all conversations, don't you!

Smiling,

Abba

*Second Corinthians 4:3-6,9-12*

Weary Worker,

A prime time for a wet blanket to smother your fire is when you are most earnestly seeking to do My bidding. It occurs when you are *pouring out your very life* to love and serve others. It happens when you are doing your gut-wrenching best. It is then that those pompous little nit-pickers appear out of nowhere and sweetly intone, "May I say something in love?"

Then, when with trembling hands and heart you smile back and mumble, "Uh, yes, please do," of course you know what is coming. And you guessed it right! You find yourself weighed in the balance and found wanting. It is a pattern nearly as predictable as sunrise and sunset.

All you have to be doing is your very best! Then suddenly, from his lofty height of piety, a self-appointed purger will swoop down and pounce on you and box your ears! You can count on it. Those critical spirits do lie in wait, just looking for opportunities to sabotage your joy. What seems worse is that I allow them to come.

And why? For one thing, I don't think you laugh enough. Not yet. I want you to develop a *robust* sense of humor, and that will happen as you learn not to take yourself too seriously. Also, I want you to find your deepest joy in My approval. The more you realize the fleeting nature of human approval, the more you will appreciate Mine.

Child, you will never rest, nor will you ever acquire deepest serenity, until you *know* that your value has nothing to do with your abilities. Your value is infinite because you belong to Infinite Love! Period. The end. Full stop!

I AM proud to report that one good thing is already surfacing in your personality. These days you nearly always think twice before you dispense *your* advice. I AM so pleased to see Christ's character forming in you!

Yours with joy everlasting,

Father

# Day 281

Faithful Restorer,

I never go back on My Word! Aren't you glad? I knew you would be. Treat others as I treat you. I will help you.

You have My wisdom within you. Shhh! Peace, cherished one! Become quiet, and you will discover it.

I AM more interested in your healing than today's happiness. You're not the only one who thinks I'm "too slow."

Last, but not least, I will never send any messenger to you who implies that I demand that you love Me more than I love you. People—or even angels—who convey such irrational messages are self-sent. You can be sure of that. The message, "God is Love, *but,*" is a lie.

With deepest understanding,

Abba

Struggling Child,

You long for purity of purpose and thought? Lavish love upon those about you! One cannot exploit and lavish love at the same time.

Until Love establishes a track record of faithfulness, trust cannot exist, let alone flourish. Don't worry about mustering faith, little one. My love delights in nurturing your heart to trust.

Faithfully, tenderly, helpfully,

Abba

Searching One,

You died in Christ and were raised with Him. His life swallows up your death. Therefore, you are to judge no one by the flesh—by external appearance—and that includes yourself. But you've forgotten that, haven't you? Never fear. My tender care will cure you.

More and more you will find yourself saying "no" to sin and "yes" to Real Life. I only ask that you receive My forgiveness when you stumble and return to My loving nurture. That is because Unconditional Love is who I AM. Therefore I show you kindness and lavish you with gifts, even when you avoid My Presence. I know that the love-seeds I AM sowing into your life will yield a harvest of holiness. Be assured, all of your old self-defeating habits will vanish as My Love heals and transforms your heart.

Already, when you look at your fellow human beings, you are noticing changes in the way you perceive them, aren't you? It is becoming increasingly difficult for you to covet any pleasure that would bring pain or ruin to someone else.

Covenant keeping, self-restraint—these qualities characterize Caring Love, and they *will* abound in you.

Remember! My commitment to you never depends on your commitment to Me. When My wayward people were "without strength" Christ died to save them, remember? That has a biblical ring to it, doesn't it?

With joy!

Your Committed Abba

*Matthew 6:7-8;*
*Romans 8:28*

Wonderful Child,

I don't mind your repeating yourself, if you find it helpful. But when you reach a stopping place, will you pause and allow Me to reply?

Today you will see Me in all things—if you will look. Savor serenity! Project peace, and astonish your friends.

Always, in joy!

Your Dad

Day 285 *Romans 8:17-18*

Daring Deliverer,

When you made up your mind to allow My Spirit to lead you, you didn't foresee this time of testing. I saw it coming, but you did not. I knew you would experience losses. I knew you would struggle through long, howling deserts of silence. I foresaw the pressures that would bombard you from without and the pain that would fester from within.

However, it was when the hard times came that you realized the cost of heeding My gentle prompting. It was then that you also discovered the strength of My commitment—and yours. Only fiery trials can evoke such discovery.

Child, I want to thank you for not giving up. You have not been rebellious or proud, but you *have* been stubborn. And I love your kind of bullheadedness! You have not been flawless, but you have been faithful. If it were not so, I would tell you.

Some people have challenged your motives; others have questioned your sanity. Even you have wrestled with uncertainty over these issues, many times! I was glad you did. Never once did I become annoyed about it. I saw the fruit that all the furor was producing in you! The challenges strengthened, the questions clarified, the pressures purified—and I AM satisfied. And you are fortified! Now we can begin the adventure!

Yours proudly,

Dad

Baffled Liberator,

I just cannot keep everyone happy; can you? If you ever stumble across a formula for making people feel comfortable and stimulated at the same time, I'd appreciate your input. Gotcha!

Smiling,

Dad

Dearest Death-Dreading Child,

It happened in about three seconds. The victim sensed only a sharp twinge of coolness, a numb impact as the floor rushed into his face, a fleeting ache mingled with swirling images—then oblivion.

John found himself on his feet, staring in silence. He watched a swordsman seize the bleeding head by its matted hair and plop it onto a large platter, which he shoved into the hands of a subordinate.

Despite his cool demeanor, the eyes of the younger soldier widened slightly, registering shock and disgust. "Somebody's got to do it!" retorted the older, wiping and re-sheathing his saber. The two strode out, bearing their gruesome trophy. Never once did they look behind them.

With calm detachment John watched the armored figures mounting the stairs that led into the darkness beyond. What was that mad music and revelry blaring in the distance? Was Herod hosting another party? Whatever it was, it hushed with the slam of another door.

John glanced around the cell. His eyes fell on the mutilated body that lay half kneeling, half sprawling at his feet. *Where am I?* John wondered. *And who was this man judged deserving of a death so brutal?*

"You are with Me now," came a Vibrant Whisper. "You are be-holding the remains of My voice in the wilderness, a man willing to decrease so that I might increase. Do you remember?"

Joy surged, and John remembered. Then he forgot.

That is, he rapidly began forgetting as gentle beings, emitting lightning radiance, appeared and surrounded him. Moments later he noticed their loving arms were somehow nudging him higher. Awestruck, John realized that he and his welcoming party were ascending stairs that spiraled ever upward into a life-transmitting radiance that no earthly tongue could describe.

*Why have I never noticed these stairs before?* John thought to himself.

As he rose into the brilliance that showered from above him, music unknown to mortal ears ravished him with unspeakable joy. The higher he ascended, the more it swelled with unbearable sweetness. Earth-memories vanished amidst the music.

What else mattered? John was home.

Yours at all times and in all worlds,

Abba

# Day 288

*Psalm 78;*
*James 3:13*

Weary Restorer,

The squeaky wheel gets the grease, true enough. But in your weary world, wheels that squeak often, despite frequent lubrication, will get ignored—or scrapped and replaced! Persistent whiners and intimidators, beware!

Talk about a wild experience! Try listening to people carping because you never go out of your way to help them, when they owe their very lives to your kindness!

I do understand,

Abba

Dearest Child,

I think you should know that many people open their hearts to you who have yet to know how to open them to others. You live in a fatherless generation, cherished one. So I AM anointing you to raise up many sons who will grow up to become true fathers in our household.

What do you think? I think I have called you! That is what I think. So I will vindicate you and open doors for you that *no one* can shut. My prophet Joel foretold that My "handmaidens" also would prophesy. I intend to fulfill that promise. Of that you can be sure.

I know you feel unworthy, little one. I can deal with that easily enough. If you considered yourself qualified, believe Me, I would be sending you an entirely different message! Stop worrying about satan's devices. No, I did not make a mistake; I refuse to capitalize the enemy's name! Of course you realize that I have no desire to insult him; it simply has always been My policy to lift up the humble and to put the proud in their place. You have observed Me do that many times, haven't you!

Seeing you smile always delights Me.

With all of My heart,

Your Dad

Worried Child,

It is error to think of satan as being the "sheer personification of evil." Evil is merely a perversion of goodness. So how could it have the substance required to be a person? The enemy is a person because I created him *before* he grew wicked. Oh yes, he now does evil, but evil is not his real substance.

Actually, satan possesses only one virtue—albeit a sadly tarnished one. He is very industrious! He is not at all lazy. Would you like to demolish his schemes? Ignore him and sing for joy! That will do it every time. I believe in you!

Your biggest fan,

Dad

Stressed Inquirer,

What is the secret of keeping people frantic? Scurrying to please? Cultivate hypersensitivity! Interpret the smallest oversight as a personal affront! Enjoy solitude—for a lifetime.

People intimidate and control because they fall prey to fear. Paranoia breeds power struggles, accusation, and slander. Rest in My embrace, child. Resign from the rat race! Trust Me to restore and vindicate.

Yours with tender concern,

Abba

Day 292

*Deuteronomy 4:29;*
*First Corinthians 13*

Lovable Explorer,

Hmmm—so you have decided to approach the question of My existence with an open mind, have you? I think you should know that you are not reading these words by accident.

Ever since you decided to abandon your "faith," I have had mixed feelings. On one hand, because your earlier perceptions of Me were so muddled (and far too religious!), I was glad to see you discard them. On the other hand, I have sorrowed for your loneliness. Having no God and believing in a false god, in the end, are equally stressful for a being created to enjoy the True and Living One.

However, I have had no choice but to honor *your* choices— at least for a season. Had I interrupted your search prematurely, you would have acknowledged Me and related to Me, but only after a fashion. In many respects you would have remained frustrated and imprisoned. You certainly would not have known how far My love would go to reach you,

Are you a bit embarrassed that I have suddenly shown up? Please don't be. I cannot hide forever behind the scenes. Treasured child, you live in My universe and *you* are an important part of it. So of course I think about you all the time!

I have "overheard" you thinking about your needing a new beginning. I was not trying to meddle; knowing everyone's thoughts just happens to be a natural "limitation" of My omniscience, so to speak. However, I think you should know that I want a new beginning for you even more than you do. I long to help you avoid another false start and to provide you with a real one.

I AM available to help you anytime you wish. I just want to let you know that.

Your Best Friend,

Abba God

P.S. I remember hearing you pray recently when you found yourself in a "tight spot." Who were you talking to?

Weeping One,

Deliverance often arrives disguised as disaster. Will you look beyond the storm and see My salvation? Right now you're seeing but one tiny snippet of a wonderful story that I have authored for your joy.

You know Me now! You understand My heart and My character. Therefore, you should know that I AM guarding all your tomorrows, as promised. You committed them to My keeping, didn't you?

Yours with eternal vigilance,

Dad

Struggling Child,

Think for a few moments about the miracles your Lord performed in His earthly ministry. He opened deaf ears and blind eyes, caused lame legs to walk, cured people of leprosy. My Son even raised the dead!

All of His miracles are packed with meaning. Have you ever thought about their implications? When He restored crippled limbs, Christ exhibited My power to heal that which is lame in the human personality—your personality. By opening blind eyes, He demonstrated My ability to give sight to the eyes of your heart. Even now, chosen conqueror, He rends the veil that blocks your vision of who I AM and of who I AM for you! In the Light of who I AM, you will discover who you are. You then will see *and know* your true identity and purpose. I promise you, child!

Soon the beauty of things you have yet to behold in their true glory will ravish you. You will see them from My perspective! Then, things you once found attractive will grow dull in your sight. You will wonder how they ever enticed you. That which is deaf in your deepest heart will flourish with sensitivity. That which leads to nowhere and is leprous and degrading in your affections will fade away like a forgotten dream.

Christ makes all things new. Yes, out of your inner being He calls forth new desires and affections, for He is the Resurrection and the Life. And He is *your* Strong Deliverer. You have not misplaced your trust! That is, not until recently.

Lately, you have hindered Heaven's work by trying to help. Tell Me, what caused you to begin that strenuous behavioral modification program? You're becoming so rigid and tense that your loved ones can hardly live with you—let alone enjoy your company!

Child, mere man-power cannot manufacture what you want. That requires a miracle that only Christ in you can perform! He is My Gift to you, and He lives inside you. Be assured, your Lord's childlike virtue will surface in your character. Your heart will be exactly like His! Your life will shine with the light of His life. That is your destiny. Be at peace about your past and how others see you. I AM! I have you *lavishly* covered by grace. Those who trust Christ will not be put to shame. I have given you My word about that, have I not? You know I have. Cease striving and strategizing, and your stress will vanish.

What do I want from you? I long for you to know beyond all question that I love you. Once My Faithful Spirit saturates your heart with that certainty, you will have crossed a frontier from which there is no return. Thankfully!

Yours, at all times and in all realms, forever!

Dad

Puzzled Conqueror,

I know you will enjoy real security when you abandon all illusions. Thus, I let this world and all its systems disillusion you, little by little. My miracle-workers just cannot invest their hopes in lost causes!

When rage erupts for having endured unreality's mad tyranny, one has reached the road to recovery. Am I glad you are mad—at long last! Now we can get on with your life.

With exuberant delight!

Dad

Perplexed Pioneer,

Of course the enemy is agitated! You're invading his turf—or so he imagines! You are taking territory he has dominated for centuries and daring to challenge his claims. Stand your ground. It is *our* ground.

I AM honoring your prayers. Thank you for trying the untried. I appreciate your refusal to conform to the so-called norms of sterile religiosity. Your courage to reveal My true heart to a hurting world *will* bear fruit. Move forward, cherished one! Refuse to retreat! Rejoice in My unfailing mercy every step of the way. Let no criticism crush your hope. Allow no bitterness to steal your joy. I have established you in the realization that you can *always* count on Me—no matter what. Rest in that realization.

Child, as experience has shown you, I do not know how to fail! Christ's blood—His very life—covers you. My Spirit anoints, indwells, and empowers you. Let love govern your heart, and you will never lack wisdom. Moreover, fear will never find a foothold in your mind.

What you want others to do to you, do to them. That is My policy. I always love My neighbors as Myself. I realize that many teachers of religion say I do not, but their traditions have blinded them to who I AM. That is why I have called you, chosen one. You will show the world who I AM—Love that *never* fails. Sing for joy!

Yours with strength everlasting,

Abba

Discouraged One,

Faithfulness is not a synonym for infallibility, little one. I rejoice in your faithfulness. Do you know why? You keep on trying! That is what matters most, in My view.

You keep putting yourself down. I keep pulling you back up. Down! Up! Down! Up! I AM patient in this because I delight in training My children. Soon you will feel more comfortable being up than down.

Love always,

Dad

Pressured Conqueror,

Thanksgiving paves the way for peace to return to your heart. Rejoice in what I *have* done for you. That will free you from torment. I want you to be happy! You may as well be, for I intend to fulfill My promises and lead you into joy.

"What has happened?" you have asked. I will tell you. You have sought to live by mere logic, and now you are getting locked into logistics. However, that is nothing new where you are concerned, is it? Never fear! The obsession to reason your way through problems, apart from listening to My Spirit inside you, will not always dominate your life. I can assure you of that.

Yes, at the moment, a "rational" devil that fosters irrational behavior gnaws away at your nerves. He would love to reason you right out of your mind! Are you going to let him? You don't have to if you don't want to, cherished one. Instead, you can relish the memories of the miracles I have already performed for you. Will you do it? Sing for joy, and I will sing with you! I have ways and means of dealing with problems that you cannot imagine.

Thanksgiving will release your spirit to receive fresh revelation and new insight. Enter in! I AM already singing joyfully over you!

Dad

# Day 299

Annoyed Toiler,

The last shall be first. The first shall be last. Why do you worry about where you'll appear in the line-up? You are already in the Kingdom, aren't you?

I know you've worked hard, and those about you appreciate your faithfulness, but sometimes people forget to say thank you. Don't worry child, I never do.

Many, many thanks!

Abba

Psalm 62:12;
Second Corinthians 8:12

Exhausted Child,

You haven't been selfish. You have given generously. What a blessing you are! Cease condemning yourself. I said it long ago, but I will say it again—I assess your giving on the basis of what you have to give, not on the basis of what you lack. This policy applies whether your gifts be financial or whether they simply consist of your labors of love. I never, never judge by the external appearance. I always, always look at heart motivation. When are you going to realize I AM not a Pharisee? Be at peace, cherished one. I delight in your willing heart.

Oh yes, I will indeed judge and reward all my children according to their works, yourself included. But aren't you glad that it is I who will do the judging? When I judge, mercy multiplies. When people judge...but you already know how that works, don't you?

While we're on the subjects of hearts, will you now allow Me to sort out some things that have been happening in your own? Don't be afraid, treasured child. Relief! That is what I have in mind for you.

I have caused you to cling to Me. It is not by your own might that you press into My Presence. No, I have drawn you to Myself. Why? I long to comfort your hurting heart with the healing warmth of Mine.

Yours with deepest tenderness,

Abba

Inquiring Conqueror,

Request granted! I AM giving you wisdom. Behave toward others as you would have them behave toward you. Expect miracles!

You've asked for My wisdom, so now you possess it. Doubting the words I've spoken to your spirit will cast you adrift upon the turbulence of human opinion. All I ask is your trust.

Trusting you always,

Dad

# Day 302

*Psalm 16:5-6;*
*Hebrews 5:14;*
*Revelation 3:7*

Cherished Child,

I have already promised to bless all of earth's families in Christ. That includes you and your family as well. So you must not allow false responsibility and worry to drive you into enterprises that I have not ordained for you. When My children buck against the boundaries I have established for them, they sabotage their own success. So please bear in mind that I open doors that no man can close, and I close doors that no man can open.

When through Scripture I told you to make the most of every opportunity, I was referring to those opportunities that I clearly provide. It was not in My heart for you to receive those words as a mandate to launch into a mad scramble to renovate the world overnight. You must learn the secret of waiting—especially at this stage of your growth. But yes, you are right. Lately I have been reining you in and frustrating your plans, which are worthy enough, but untimely. Please do not blame others for hindering your ministry. The blame, as it were, is Mine.

I love you too much to lose you to religiosity. That cruel treadmill would only bring you exhaustion and grief. As I have told you, I have the highest aspirations regarding your destiny.

Yours patiently,

Your loving Abba

Frantic Restorer,

Saving up for a rainy day? What if it never rains until the year 2187? Consider the lilies. Think of My sparrows. Beware of battling monsters that appear only in daydreams!

My resourcefulness defies imagination! Refuse to let appearances steal your hope. Paranoia perceives only the surface of things. Faith laughs at lying illusions!

Yours faithfully,

Abba

Dearest Child,

Bear in mind that love looks for ways to believe the best about others. Love does not delight in exposing sin, nor does it rejoice when another fails. If I kept a record of wrongs, who could possibly stand? But Mine is a forgiving heart. That is why you treasure Me and hold Me in highest esteem. I so appreciate that. You keep telling others how My unconditional love has healed you and freed you to live in hope. And it is true, isn't it? I have won your deepest admiration because I have loved you no matter what, come what may. It is My kindness that has transformed your thoughts and behavior, your very life.

Do you yearn for others to respect and love you? I know you do, cherished one. So throw away your list of infractions! Forgive those who have hurt you and choose to forget their failures. Let us overcome evil with good. I will help you.

No human being can thwart the wonderful plans I have for you. Trust My relentless love. Hope in My power! Ravishing you with joy brings Me sheer delight, and you can count on Me to protect you. No evil can harm you! You have no reason to worry. Do you see it, little one? Neither your future nor that of your loved ones depends on people. I AM your Provider, your Protector, your Promoter, your Almighty Father and Closest Friend. Your future depends on Me!

Many thanks for your trust!

Dad

Weeping Child,

Help is on the way. I know you are hurting. It's not against the rules to cry in our family. I love kissing away tears. I know your pain. I cry with you. Lean on Me and remember My power. I AM your Rock of Refuge and your Ally. I know your anguish, and I promise—no evil will triumph over you! I will see to it.

Holding you close,

Abba

Harassed Child,

When carping words come to wound you, bear in mind that I will defend you. I see to it that people who lay down the law to others are themselves laid low by the law. Oh yes, of that you can be sure! I make certain that they entangle themselves in their own talk, sooner or later. What else can I do? I have no choice! It is just the way things work in the Kingdom of Heaven. It is a spiritual principle. It is not that I particularly enjoy nabbing nit-pickers and outmaneuvering manipulators. But who else knows the rules well enough to outwit them—to show them reality? You certainly do not. Furthermore, I don't expect you be your own defense attorney.

Let Me work the rules! Trust Me to vindicate you. I have proven Myself able, have I not? As you well know, your Good Shepherd and I have interesting ways of tenderizing the hearts of hardheaded people. We even know how to make them happy while we do so!

Do you recall how your Strong Deliverer nabbed Saul of Tarsus? In a single moment your Lord reduced that opinion-ated rebel to a quivering heap at His feet! Saul became known as Paul thereafter. Moreover, he became one of Heaven's most notable friends. As Paul himself would tell you, I AM extremely resourceful!

Your Mighty Fortress always,

Dad

Brave Warrior,

Satan always plots to seduce you just after you've performed exploits. So, what else is new? Down with the devil! Let's laugh! Our laughter annihilates lust.

Thank you for saying yes to Me and no to the evil one. You've spared not only us, but also many others from much heartache. Heaven rejoices for your courage!

Yours with delight,

Abba

Faithful One,

I want to thank you for supporting My weaker child. I have seen your many hours of constant caring and how you have devoted your time and substance. Oh yes. I have known when others have not. Time and again I have watched as you have forsaken your own sorrow and labored on to comfort another who is confused and badly broken. So again, thank you. You have been a friend—My friend—in the truest sense of the word. Please know I will not forget your sacrifices. How could I?

Yes, I know. Certain ones who should know better (yet who prefer to remain at a comfortable distance) have hinted that your labors of love could ruin your reputation. It has even been sweetly suggested that people might identify you with the shame of sins not your own. And some who are far "holier" than I AM have denounced your efforts, saying your work has brought dishonor to Christ.

However, your Lord and I have discussed these things at great length, and He doesn't have a clue of what they're talking about! On the other hand, We both know *exactly* what your critics are talking about—and it is not about you. It is about them. Of course, they have yet to realize it.

Just remember, your reputation will stand or fall with Mine. So why worry about it? So what if we have become "of no reputation"? Tenderhearted one, I have gone this route before, believe Me, and there is nothing like a timely resurrection to revive a tarnished reputation! Be of good cheer. All the clamor and commotion will cease with the grand promotion I have planned for you.

Then you will discover how many friends you have had all along, won't you? Yes, you'll have yet another opportunity to forgive and forget, but join the club! I do it all the time.

With all of My heart,

Abba

*Philippians 4:19;*
*Colossians 1:9*

Searching Child,

My Spirit longs to flood you with light, illuminating the eyes of your spirit to perceive My will. Why should I play hide and seek with you? Wanting My will is having it! My Spirit lives inside you! I do abundantly above and beyond all you can ask or imagine. Remember who and Whose you are!

In joy,
Your Abba

# Day 310

Deliberating Conqueror,

Balaam the prophet was so bent on doing his own thing that when his donkey began talking to him, he failed to notice the incongruity. He retorted instantly, as if conversing with an animal were an event as normal as scratching his nose! Poor Balaam. His selfish heart had so obsessed his mind that the wonder of a talking donkey eluded him completely. The man was too blind to see the sun in the sky. Far less could he perceive that he had lost touch with the Spirit of revelation and that I had anointed his worthy beast instead! Alas, such is the nature of greed. *Ambitious minds always miss miracles.*

Jonah had a similar problem. He too was My prophet, but he got it in his mind that he was more spiritual than Yours Truly. When I commissioned him to warn the Ninevites of My coming judgment, he knew I would spare them if they repented. So he balked! Jonah had no love for the people I yearned to save. Moreover, he preferred to enjoy the approval of his biased peers over having Mine. So he tried to run away. My beloved but stubborn prophet flatly rejected My call.

So? I found a vessel that *would* respond—a fine and frolicsome fish! As you know, I have never had a problem with animals. Those noble and pure creatures, from the least to the greatest, all delight to do My bidding. I have commissioned cows to transport My Covenant Ark. I have inspired frogs, locusts, and flies to change the mind of a proud king. The fish I sent to swallow up my prejudiced prophet Jonah also did an excellent job of persuasion. Do you recall?

I know this has been a "beastly" revelation, in a manner of speaking. However, I just thought it would be good to remind you that I can anoint anyone or anything I choose. Furthermore, all that I desire to occur *will* come to pass. Whatever I purpose *will* happen.

Thank you for refusing to compromise your calling. Thank you for avoiding the agendas of religious people who are short-sighted and selfish. I appreciate your choosing to walk the path of love—no matter what the cost. Thank you for doing what I have called you to do and for being who I have called you to be. Yes, treasured one, I realize that, to some degree, I AM thanking you in advance for your obedience. However, as I recall, you often thank Me in advance for answering your prayers, don't you?

I love our transparent relationship.

Your omnipotent Dad

Isaiah 40:31;
Psalm 145:8-9;
First Corinthians 13:8

Perplexed Questioner,

What happens to those who hope in Me? To those who wait in My Presence? They grow strong in body and spirit. Like eagles, they soar above the world's chaos. They run without weariness. They can walk and walk and walk and yet never succumb to despair.

Prophecies may fail, yet Love never fails. Peace, cherished one. You are My creation and My tender mercies are over all My works.

Always and forever,

Dad

*Ephesians 4:1-16*

My Valiant Defender,

Sometimes I subject your ears to voices expounding doubtful doctrines. Do you know why? I appoint imperfect people as Heaven's demolition agents to explode the illusion of perfectionism and to irritate those who promote it. Perfectionism hinders true holiness.

Each time idolatry of intellect makes love with pride of appearance, another devil (accuser!) is born. I allow imperfect people to bungle about in our house so that laughter can render such cohabitation ridiculous! Holy mirth dismantles pride, leaving idolatry without a lover.

By the way, I have missed hearing your joy-generating wisecracks. I think they're wonderful!

Honestly,

Abba

Searching Disciple,

Avoid analysts-paralysis, and savor the supernatural! Ask My Holy Spirit for the words you should pray. He will grant them! Do you realize that when you pray in the Spirit, you are joining with Me to plunder the dominion of darkness? When our hearts harmonize, nothing can oppose the power of our words!

I have blessed your eyes with supernatural vision and your ears with miraculous hearing. Will you dare to use them? Trust Me to cover and guide you.

Always your Rock of Refuge,

Abba

Dear Truth-Seeker,

Never underestimate My ingenuity! I have ways of showing up in your life that would boggle your mind. You have demanded that I prove My existence and My love for you. I have no intention of letting that demand go unchallenged.

But of course! You can count on it. I always act and respond in ways that you could never foresee. I love to surprise you. That is why My friends who know Me, heart-to-heart, find Me interesting, believe it or not. However, you tend to think I'm dreary and dull. I don't blame you for that. The pompous little god that joyless religiosity advertises bores Me too! Since your concept of who I AM came from that source, I could not agree with you more. The idea of "God" that you (thus far) have acquired truly is dreary and dull.

Angry? Why should I be angry? Many of My children have a muddled perception of Me. It would be absurd to take personal offense in their case or in yours. People can only know what they know. That is, until I show up!

Yours sincerely,

Dad

# Day 315

Frustrated Child,

I only "hassle" the people I love. Do you think I enjoy scrambling the schedules of My squawking children? I'm bailing you out. Consider yourself rescued! Passivity paralyzes. Paralyzation invites victimization. Have you ever heard of a "sitting duck"?

Enter into Life, child! Then Life's purpose will emerge with splendor, laughing every quibbling question into irrelevance! Your trust would be appreciated.

Helpfully,

Dad

Thoughtful Child,

You have wondered about hell. *Hell* is a word that means "grave." I AM Love Personified. From My point of view, people who do not know Me do not know Love. They are dead—spiritually dead. They are in *grave* condition. When people refuse the Light of My Love, I must allow them to remain in spiritual death—as long as they prefer it. Of course, that doesn't mean I give up on them. After all, I sent My Son into the world to raise the dead!

Have I ever given up on you? Certainly not! I know the pain that festers inside you and how it originates from your wrong perception of who I AM. I just want you to know that I AM available and that I AM your Closest Friend. So you can enjoy My company anytime you wish. Only dare to become quiet, and listen to your heart.

Not one moment passes that I do not think of you. Not one! Soon I will confirm this fact by a small miracle of supply. You will not be able to explain the arrival of this gift in any other way than that I dropped it "out of the sky."

What a wonderful smile you have! I like it.

Your Real Dad

Scrambling Worker,

No man is busier than the one protecting his "rights." You look exhausted. I AM slowing you down today. This is making our world a friendlier place—if only by a fraction. Are you rejoicing? I AM answering your prayers for sanity. Also for a loving heart.

Ever thinking of you,

Abba

Dear Child,

Here I AM again! It delights Me to show up for you at just the right time. I know My sudden appearances often surprise you, and I AM also aware how they sometimes annoy you.

I don't always seem interested in the issues you would like to address, do I? Instead, I begin sounding off about My dreams for you; or about repentance; or of the need to forgive others; or about the benefits of patience, commitment, trust—you name it! I show up out of the blue and begin talking about anything and everything but the topic you have in mind.

Cherished one, I regret that My ways frustrate you on occasions. If it pleases you, you can attribute them to My old age. I have been around for a very long time! However, you have another option. You might ask yourself *why* the issues that consume all of your attention seem more important to you than what I have to say.

Yes, in a sense you are right. In a manner of speaking, I AM turning your little world upside down at the moment. Actually, I AM doing you a favor. Bit by bit, I'm dismantling a false world and giving you a real one! Once the dust settles, I think you will be greatly relieved.

Simplicity, order, sanity, a solid sense of significance and purpose. You have yearned for these, have you not? Yes, and I have yearned even more that you have them. Your pain matters to Me. You matter to Me, far more than you can imagine.

Thank you for trusting,

Dad

Burdened Child,

Satan does not share equal power with Me! Evil is a parasite. Our laughter can dislodge it in an instant, have you noticed?

Whatever power your enemies may wield, I will free you from their tyranny. Enjoy the spacious place I give you by grace. I help you, not because you always deserve it, but because I love you!

Always,

Your Dad

Questioning Child,

When I first confirmed to you that your prayers had reached My ears, I knew you would need additional encouragement later on. Don't worry about symptoms! What appears to you as your difficulty returning is actually the reverse. The affliction is no longer working its way inside of you. Now it is working its way out.

Sing for joy! Delight in Me, cherished conqueror, as I delight in you. Cease analyzing and scrutinizing that which is on its way out; plunge into your new life, and enjoy!

You may as well take the plunge now, for—whatever happens—I will complete all I have begun in you. So why not choose to be happy? I AM!

Loving you with fierce devotion,

Abba

Weeping Warrior,

The law of life flourishing in Jesus frees you from the law of sin and destruction! Everlasting life. Life indestructible! Life impervious to attack or erosion that brings My healing to a hurting world. Such life you possess forever through Jesus!

Why aren't you rejoicing? Why are you dreading backlash from your blunders? Resume walking with Me! Our fellowship will foster improved performance—in time.

Love,

Dad

Recovering Restorer,

You already know this, but I will tell you again. I oppose promiscuity that calls itself "freedom" because I know that it is *not* freedom; it is bondage. I know the heartache it brings.

I AM Unfailing Love, true enough, and I AM glad you realize that. Even so, I cannot be a responsible Father and at the same time cancel all negative consequences in our universe. Often I can modify them, and in My mercy I do so. Yet even then many of My children reap a harvest of untold agony simply because they have ignored *reality*.

Please, treasured child, make it easy on yourself and on My tender heart for you. Do anything wholesome and fun, but flee fornication. I want you to enjoy your life! Living in lust will render that impossible, sooner or later. It will cause *real* happiness to elude you. Giving free rein to your passions will only bring you pain and regret.

Yes, I will confirm—the lights have come on, so to speak. Child, you are now seeing that most of your mental anguish has been self-imposed. So our task is to retrain your brain, isn't it? As astonishing as it seems, I can assure that you have *fun* while I renew your mind. That is because your thought patterns heal and your cravings change as you learn the simple joy of walking and talking with Me. In other words, your restoration will come as I impart increasing revelation to your heart.

You will see! More and more I will show you who I AM, who you are, and what our lives are all about. These revelations will become *solid realities* in your deepest being. I will bless and amaze you with knowledge—vivid and detailed—that will inspire faith in many doubt-darkened hearts. Even now in the midst of your struggles you are My healing light. Yes, that's who you are and I love seeing you shine!

Live in My healing embrace and you will always shine. Cease worrying about your weaknesses. My Presence empowers you to love everyone with a pure heart. I will protect you fiercely and will provide for you lavishly. Haven't I always?

Thank you for caring. Thank you for counting on Me and rejecting religion's lie of conditional love. Have you ever wondered Who inspired you to do that?

Humbly yours forever,

Abba

Curious Child,

Just some food for thought: Are you a Christian? Test: When another person falters, do you spread the word or do you weep?

I refuse even to address suspicions. Another's frailties are none of your business! I enjoy singing, not snooping. Any more questions?

Yours with fierce loyalty,

Abba

# Day 324

Chosen Liberator,

Rejoice! You have nothing to fear. Refuse to confuse mere appearances with realities. I AM now answering the heart-cry of all who yearn for deliverance. As you recall, Christ is My Healing Light, and He is committed to shine on all who weep in darkness. That is why the world's totems are toppling and corrupt religious systems are crumbling. These are not catastrophes, child. They are indicators of the Light of My Glory increasing worldwide!

As the bogus gods of earth and their lying illusions disintegrate, people begin searching for the True and Living God. This describes your own experience, does it not? The time came when you "lost" everything, including your reputation. Then you decided to trust Me with your future and public image. You also chose to rely on Me for your provision. So now you have nothing to lose. Isn't that wonderful? No earthly care can oppress you because, at last, you have a life!

As chaotic as circumstances appear, My radiant Redeemer Son—as never before—is infusing *life* into the world. Do you recall that I have committed all judgment into your Good Shepherd's hands? I have done that, not to destroy My lost sheep, but to restore them. It is time that they become all that I have longed for them to be. The world-weary *will* come to their senses. When they do, they will deeply honor and adore your Lord and Myself for our kindness in freeing them from their destroyers. They will no longer cherish the idols that only brought them pain.

Child, you now are free. Things no longer possess you. People's opinions no longer rob you of sleep. Hasn't that caused you to love Me all the more? Indeed it has. Surely you know that your increased devotion has not escaped My notice!

That is why it has been My delight to empower *you* as never before to infuse life into our world—to shatter the shackles of despair. My Light shines through you and from you with amazing energy that heals broken hearts.

Just remember that you cannot expect to transmit My Spirit's power and go unchallenged. Increased power is bound to stir up even more opposition. That is the simple reality of reigning in our Kingdom. At least, at present it is. But didn't I hear you say that you wanted to be in the midst of the action? I AM certain I heard you say so—more than once. Well, here you are!

Why not be at peace about it and enjoy our work together? I AM!

Forever yours,

Dad

Treasured Conqueror,

Stop rehearsing defenses and arguments! You do not need them now nor will you need them later. You have Me, and that's enough. You'll see.

I repeat. Refuse to worry in advance how you will defend yourself. I will give you words of wisdom that will stun your adversaries into silence!

With pleasure!

Abba

Trusted Restorer,

I share your concerns. Any parrot of average intelligence can learn to talk. We both know that clever humans can learn to wrangle over words and their meanings. However mere rhetoric and logic are powerless to heal hurting people at the deepest level, and we both know that as well. "Laying down the law" and even backing it up with the Bible only fosters more pain and rebellion. Do you remember Romans, chapter seven? What about your own journey? Do you recall your struggles? *Words **alone** just cannot heal.* Nor can the loftiest law generate life.

It is My power—Love's Energy—that spawns new creations! Principles, formulas, and instructions cannot raise the dead. That is why I did not send a textbook into the world; I sent My Son. He came to heal the brokenhearted! He did *not* come to explain to them how to heal themselves in 666 easy steps that actually are *not* so easy. I'm tired of religious "How To" seminars, aren't you?

Anyone can spout off logical-sounding noises. Anyone can expose error or point an accusing finger. But where are My deliverers who transmit the healing power of My love?

If I seem angry, that is because I'm passionate about people. I'm done with smug-sounding semantics that reek of the refuse of self-righteousness while parading themselves as "the gospel."

My heart aches because many of My chosen co-heirs have no clue as to *why* I have called them out of darkness into My marvelous Light. I have anointed them to be a royal priesthood to serve and intercede for a lost world. I yearn for them to impart My Power—Love's power! Only *that* will cause the tyrannical governments seated in hell's gates to crumble!

I have not called out My priesthood people to "go to Heaven" to the exclusion of the rest of the world. I have called them out to *bring* Heaven to everyone, everywhere. I have called out a healing family of co-regents who will not fail or give up until My deliverance transforms the world! The earth is Mine in all of its fullness—*and* those who dwell in it. And it is yours, cherished conqueror. Oh yes, I do mean that. The world is yours for the taking, if you want it. Do you want to abandon it? To use it? Or to heal and transform it?

Do you yearn to see Love fill everything and everyone everywhere? I think you do. So go, healing warrior! Set the captives free! I live inside you. My Son Light illuminates your path. You are filled with Love's energy, so you *will* go in My power, be assured!

I AM supporting you, backing you, empowering you every step of the way!

With sheer delight,

Abba

Delightful Child,

Humans arrive in so many shapes and colors! Don't you find them interesting? Bigotry blinds. Love enlightens. People who are ever looking for ways to love are always performing miracles. Of course, they would roar with laughter if anyone told them that!

Yours with joy,

Abba

P.S. A myriad of options surround you. Thanksgiving will open your eyes to see them.

Chosen Deliverer,

I don't mind telling you again. Any thought that impairs your hope does not come from Me. Please remember that. You are not in a position to properly assess your success. I have designed you to live in revelation, not to be locked into a prison of mere information. That is why I tell you that you must not judge anything or anyone by outward appearance—including yourself.

Righteous judgment almost never bears even a faint resemblance to the conclusions that people reach when analyzing themselves or others. The truth—the whole truth—contains too many factors for the mortal mind to grasp.

For example, in your limited vision the earth appears flat. However, we both know it is round. Even so, it looks flat because your physical eyes can perceive only a small part of the whole.

The same holds true for your view of success. Believe Me, if I suddenly caused your life to conform to your present concept, that picture would soon fail to please you. I can assure you of that, child. Have you forgotten? I know you! I know you better than you know yourself.

So it all comes back to trusting Me, doesn't it? You already know that nothing less than childlike faith can please Me. Yet, here is another thought for you to consider: doubt and unbelief make *you* impossible to please. (Your loved ones will be happy to confirm this if you ask them.)

Now, just to encourage you...I know that you've thought your recent prayers were selfish and vain, but they were not. Not only did you pray in harmony with My will, My Spirit empowered and inspired your petitions. Consider them granted! Soon you will discover that My range of interests far exceeds what you have imagined. I think it is time to begin broadening your thinking.

Yours with joy,

Dad

P.S. Keep this message a secret, will you? Some of My children are too steeped in religious tradition to appreciate My policies at present.

*Psalm 118:21-24;*
*John 6:28-29*

Cherished Child,

Are you going to let this day intimidate you? Jesus is the Everlasting Holiday I have provided for you. Rejoice, and be glad in Him!

How can you accomplish the works of God? Rely on Jesus. Believe in Jesus. Trust in Jesus. Look to Jesus. Rest in Jesus, receiving His loving nurture, and of course, by putting His words into action.

Yours with all power,

Dad

Hurting Child,

You need to know that I *never* give advice that I do not follow Myself. Nor do I command anything that I cannot carry out in My own Life. I will never require something of you that I Myself do not possess. Little one, that would make Me worse, by far, than a hypocrite. Such a contradiction in My character would make Me a lunatic! How could I teach others what I do not know? How could I be rational and just and yet demand that you show mercy that would be greater than Mine?

You are not wrong to disbelieve in the irrational god of man-made religion. Those who believe in him (it!) become irrational themselves. My commands are My commitments. They are what I Myself commit to uphold. Bearing this in mind, consider what the following commands/commitments say about Me:

- What you would have others do to you, do also to them.

- Be angry and sin not.

- Do not let the sun go down on your wrath.

- Give cheerfully!

- Always forgive, even if it comes to forgiving 70 times 7 times—daily!

- Be thankful in all things.

- Love your enemies, and bless those who curse you.

- Refuse to return evil for evil, but instead overcome evil with good.

Cherished one, I AM hoping that as you ponder these commands, you will realize that they are a description of who I AM. Christ came not to contradict, but to fulfill the law and the prophets. These are summed up in the words, "You shall love your neighbor as yourself." Aren't you His little neighbor? And Mine?

You are right. It is impossible to love and admire a god that is less compassionate than you are. Any "theology" that advertises such a god deserves the garbage heap. I'm glad we agree on the basics of sound doctrine.

Loving you always!

Abba

Day 331

*Colossians 2:8-9;*
*James 4:7*

Exhausted Child,

How can one detect the absence of true holiness? By the presence of any oppression that exterminates hope, simplicity, trust, caring love. Beware! Grace exterminators usually arrive disguised as proclaimers of "holiness."

Devils just will not submit to reason! Why do you think Heaven gave them the boot? You do likewise!

Yours, all powerfully,

Dad

*Matthew 6:25-34;*
*Ephesians 3:20*

Cherished Restorer,

I repeat! I know you better than you know yourself. What you think you want is often different from what you truly want in your heart of hearts. That is why, as your Loving Father, I must exercise sound judgment and at times say "no" to your requests. Actually, I AM not ignoring your desires. As experience has already taught you, I AM working to grant your *deepest* desires.

Your real needs are what matter in the long run. Don't you agree? I AM considering your real needs even now in response to your prayers for promotion. I hope you'll not mind My asking, but are you ready for this change you seek?

As we've discussed before, treasured one, it is not wise to judge by the outward appearance of things. A baby bear appears cuddly and winsome, and he is—when he is a mere cub. Living with him after he has grown up is a different matter! But I'm sure you already know that. We both love animals, so I trust you will "bear" with Me as I remind you of My good intentions.

Hmmm... A "more dignified public image." You aren't serious about that, are you? Living up to an image has never satisfied you before. In My humble opinion, child, you've always been too hopelessly real for that, too down-to-earth for that. I know you. Have you forgotten? I formed you!

Calm down, treasured one. Allow Me to help you have a fresh look at your life and your deepest aspirations and calling. Lately you have drifted out of touch with *yourself*—your true self, that is. How do you expect Me to fulfill your requests when you have no clue of what you are really asking for?

I love you!
Dad

ABBA CALLING

Day 333

Pressured Child,

Before you go to bed, don't forget to take out the garbage. After you take it out this time, will you leave it out?

And please...it doesn't matter, it doesn't matter, it just doesn't matter! Peace, little one. All that matters is us.

Yes, it appears that you and I are stuck with each other. I AM not complaining about it, are you?

Yours with deepest delight,

Dad

Wrestling Warrior,

You must learn not to speculate about My opinions without first inquiring of Me. How would you feel if you stood among your friends and they theorized and talked about you as though you were absent? Would your heart ache if they deliberated and devised how to spend your money? What if they kept piping up about what they thought you might desire or think, and yet it never occurred to them to ask *you* personally? That is how much of the Church treats Me.

They come together for what they call a "prayer meeting" or a "service," and what a strange event it is! My friends mindlessly turn to Me and parrot a few memorized words and clichés. But after that? They conduct themselves as though I were nonexistent!

Is it any wonder that most church meetings bore Me? To say nothing of boring My intimate friends who know Me as a real Person! Such rigmarole not only bores them; it grieves them. It grieves them even more than it does Me. But that is just how close friends are with each other, isn't it? I would much prefer that someone hurt Me rather than one of My friends. And, of course, that is how My friends feel when people dishonor Me. I know you can relate to what I AM saying.

Cherished one, you keep asking that I become more real to you. May I tell you a secret? When you begin treating Me as a real Person, you will discover—beyond all doubt—that I AM a real Person. However, as long as you do all of the talking and none of the listening, I will always seem unreal to you.

Dare to quiet your heart, dear child, and listen more often. Cease theorizing, speculating, and reasoning. I AM ever present. Allow Me to be Myself.

I have missed your company.

Your devoted Abba

Frenzied One,

Later on I'll address the issue you want to talk about. Right now, I want to talk about our fellowship. Do you really believe that taking time for us will delay the help you are seeking? When you are already doing your best, don't worry about running "late" sometimes. As you well know, I never do. And never have I wasted a moment!

Affectionately,

Abba

P.S. Peace, tender one. i am with you! Be still, and know i am God.

# Day 336

*Ephesians 4:6*

Valiant Deliverer,

You indeed are a co-savior and co-heir with Christ. However, you are not *the* Savior. You are a co-laborer with Him. Isn't that a relief to know? I AM your diligent Father and the Manager of the cosmos. I AM above all, through all, and in all. I *work* above all, through all, and in all. So give yourself a break, child. Please...give all of us a break! You are not in control. I AM. In this truth you must rest—and rejoice and be glad. I AM a Restorer. With all due humility, I AM the Restorer above all restorers. I never begin a work that I do not bring to breathtaking, glorious perfection. Never!

Again, child, any thought that tortures your mind and prods you into frantic self-reliance does *not* come from My Spirit. Any thought that drives you into despair comes from the evil one. I allow challenges to arise in your life to deepen your trust, not to harass or hurt you. So cheer up! We—you and I—are on the right track. Furthermore, we are on schedule. Your loved one is also on schedule—exactly.

So why do I often keep you in a tilt position? It is so that you will lean on Me, of course! I'm training you to rest in hope, for it is in such repose that you *experience* the joy-radiant Life that is your portion.

As for the wisdom you have sought—yes! Request granted. Consider it done! I have told you this before, but I don't mind telling you again. Be honest. Be gracious also. Let your *yes* be yes and your *no* be no.

Keep it just that simple! Gently yet firmly refuse to yield to seduction or unrighteous compromise. Always seek to transmit caring love, and you will never stray far from wisdom. I will see to that. Thank you for taking time for us! I love you.

> With all of My heart,
>
> Your omnipotent Dad

Struggling Shepherd,

You have My approval. Why do you demand universal acceptance? Not even I enjoy that. My Self-giving love shown at Calvary makes you worthy. You are of infinite worth! Legalistic religion seduces people, causing them to spend their lifetimes toiling for what I've already given them!

Yours with a smile,

Abba

Harassed Deliverer,

Your friends do not love you for how holy you look or for how attractive, rich, or successful you are. They love you because you are you. Child, they love the person I have made you to be. Would you be happy with friends who loved you for any other reason? Of course not. So why fret about the fleeting opinions of people who don't even know you?

You are My temple, My house. I live inside you. Simply rely on Me, and the radiance of My holiness will shine from you. I have not called you to earn brownie points or to keep up appearances. I detest such straw spirituality! Many traditions that legalists esteem as sacred, I regard as refuse! I AM looking for hearts that will reflect the Light of Christ, My Self-Giving Son. His is My kind of holiness. It is the kind that appears "unholy" to those who care only about appearances.

So you want to be perfect, do you? Wonderful! Then do what I do. Shower healing grace on imperfect people. Pour your heart out to love the disreputable-looking ones in our world. Comfort the outcasts. Be friends with the nobodies. Nurture and restore those who fail. Help heal the abused—as well as their imprisoned abusers. Cherish and honor people who a sanctimonious church and a hard-nosed world care nothing about. Hold them in your arms. Cry with them. Love and assist them *always*—even if you never see your prayers for their healing answered in this lifetime.

Then—and only then—will you begin to be perfect as I AM. Thank you for resigning from the religious rat race.

I love you!
Dad

# Day 339

Weary One,

My children will never feel secure in My love until they know I walk what I talk. Forgiving seventy times seven daily was My idea. Keep on loving, forgiving, and showing mercy. I do! Where would anyone be if I didn't?

Tenderly,

Your Dad

Restless One,

Shhh! Settle down. Quiet your heart. Trust Me. I know where we are going. I have promised to protect you. I will shield you from all harm, never fear. Just make yourself at home in My Presence. I AM your Defense, so be assured—all accusations will come to naught, and all opposition will vanish.

Meanwhile, savor the tranquility that comes when you take refuge in Me. Why do you imagine that I'm reluctant to help you? It is not in My nature to give grudgingly. I delight to support you! I realize that I seem "slow" from your point of view. And yes, you are right. I never fret about time. As you well know, I AM a shrewd Strategist, and I do have surprising ways of rearranging schedules. Have you noted how I have rearranged yours? I even made time for you to receive this brief message, didn't I?

I AM smiling with you!

Dad

John 3:16;
*Second Corinthians 12:9-10;*
*Ephesians 1:17-23; First John 4:4*

Frustrated Trooper,

I knew exactly what I was getting into when I chose you! In your weakness My strength is made perfect. Keep walking. Be kind to yourself. Refuse bondage! Remember who you are, child. You pack astonishing power. Use it!

I regard you as more than ample reward for My efforts. Isn't it caring for people that counts, more than anything else in life? I'm glad we agree.

Love always,

Dad

Recovering Conqueror,

Thank you for joining forces with Me to comfort and heal the world-wounded. Even now our ministry is touching many people you will never meet until death fades forever in the unrelenting light of true life. Rest assured! All who received healing hope through your labors will come to thank you one day. They will weep for joy for having the honor at last of meeting you personally.

You still wrestle with sorrow, I know. You think that if only you had tried harder, those days of chaos would not have come. Perhaps so, if you had tried harder, cherished one. But you did not. And why? Because you could not! You gave everything you had. If anyone knows that, I do. *I* rejoice for all that you have given and done!

Will you please hear My heart? I AM not angry. You have not disappointed Me, nor am I punishing you. I AM preparing you. I AM restoring and refurbishing you for a ministry that far surpasses what you have accomplished thus far.

Do you recall those tearful times when you pleaded that I empower you to defeat the dark forces that relentlessly tortured your mind? I do. Cherished one, at this very moment I AM answering your prayers. Of course, by way of confirmation, I AM only telling you what you already know.

Just keep looking to Me. If certain ones cast a critical eye your way, what is that to us? It doesn't matter. Unhappy people steeped in joyless judgementalism just cannot hurt you if only you will keep your eyes—your attention and focus—on Me.

Thank you for allowing Me to lead you along a painful path. It was a necessary one, and now you can see why. The people I have placed in your life also can see why. It is gloriously evident to those you now touch that your journey into despair was for *their* blessing.

You have no idea how much joy you bring to My heart.

Your devoted Dad

P.S. You perceive My signals more often than you think. Why do I whisper? Your spirit yearns for the serenity of Mine.

Psalm 105:3-7; 144:1;
Isaiah 25:6-8; First Thessalonians
5:18; Revelation 5:13; 21:1-5

Impatient Conqueror,

Today you're learning the secret of savoring contentment in every situation. Delightful, isn't it?

Rely on My loving wisdom and trust My timing. If I enjoyed seeing you suffer, I would scrap preparation and grant you promotion—as requested! What kind of Father do you imagine Me to be?

Yours compassionately,

Dad

P.S. Can you imagine a world without sorrow, tears, death, separation or pain? I can.

# Day 344

Isaiah 40:31;
John 14:12;
First Corinthians 1:9

Loving Liberator,

Learn to rely on My wisdom and leading. I long to help hurting people, just as you do. However, grief sometimes rages in human hearts with such mind-binding intensity that words (any words—good, bad, or indifferent) tend only to increase their torment. More often than not, your loving presence and silent prayers supply all that is needed.

Who you are—what a magnificent gift! You, child, are a healing light to many wounded hearts, though you do not see or know how. If it were not true, believe Me, I would not say so. My Spirit dwells inside you! Shouldn't I know the Gift that I AM in you?

One day you will prophesy with astounding accuracy! You will possess power to open blind eyes and deaf ears. Furthermore, you will be able to heal crippled people, cure the hopelessly insane, raise the dead—and even renovate worlds! You will know how to be in one place and then suddenly appear in another. The weather will change at your command. You will even be able to walk on water.

You will consistently tell the truth, and always love and forgive others. Moreover, you will always understand and appreciate My thoughts and respond to My voice—without fail! And according to Jesus, your Lord, you will do even greater works than He did. Glories await you that no mortal eye can see, no natural ear can hear, and no finite mind can imagine!

Are you interested? Spend more time with Me and leave the future to Me.

Dad

Faithful One,

Yours is a heart overflowing with kindness for others. When you need mercy, do you think I will reward your gentleness with punishment? Unthinkable!

Thank you for going an extra mile! Now you've got them wondering what in Heaven's name you're up to!

Ha!

Dad

Questioning Child,

You are right. I show up when I please and I disappear when I please! I do *exactly* what I want to do—all of the time. The same is true of My Spirit, who moves like the wind, and of My Son, the Lion of Judah. And while we're on the subject of lions...

I enjoy cats of all kinds, have you noticed? People tend to love them or hate them. There is almost no middle ground in the way human beings respond to felines. Some find them annoying; others find them delightful. However, nearly everyone agrees that those clever creatures seem independent and proud.

Shall I, as they say, "let the cat out of the bag"? I think I deserve at least the same treatment that people give to the common house cat. Love Me or hate Me! I mean that. I prefer being disliked over being ignored or patronized—anytime!

Child, why should I not come and go as I please? Where were you when I designed the galaxies? In My heart, of course; that's where you were! You were nestled in there with My deepest affections. Your highest good will be forever at the heart of My actions, My policies, My comings and goings.

Never fear! I do have limits. Have you ever thought about that? Perfect Love *must* do what It wants. That is because Love always wants the very best for those It cherishes. Aren't you glad? I AM not as far away as you think.

With deepest devotion,

Your Real Dad

Cherished Child,

Mercy! Just think for a moment. What incredible kindness I shower upon you daily! Is there any reason why today should be different?

Not by might, nor by power, but by My Spirit you will conquer! It doesn't annoy Me to remind you. Start again! Call the other attempts practice. I have all of the time in all worlds for you, child.

Yours with eternal commitment,

Dad

# Day 348

Inquiring Child,

Am I ever depressed? Funny that you should ask. To answer that question, I think I should remind you that I deal with an astronomical number of factors and issues. At all times and in all realms—past, present, and future—I oversee and sustain multiple billions of people, worlds, and creatures. At every moment I care for them individually, and at every moment I also care for them corporately.

Never fear, cherished one; such labor never depresses Me. I perform these functions as easily as a man might wiggle his toes in his sleep! One could say that I manage our multi-dimensional cosmos by instinct. I AM not aware of any effort involved. That is, I never feel any stress from My work. So, in an overall sense, I never experience depression. Wouldn't we all be in deep trouble if I did? I cannot be anything less than Almighty God, because I AM simply what and who I AM—all-pervading Joy, unfailing Holy Love.

However, at times some situations do sadden a part of My heart. For example, I grieve for the deception and pain of people who refuse to receive My love. My heart aches when My wayward children recognize truth yet choose to build their lives on lies. I weep also for all who are abused, afraid or lonely, burdened or suffering.

May I be utterly honest? Sometimes your depression does depress Me a bit, so to speak. For example, you and I enjoy an intimacy that My prophets of old would have envied. As a result, you live in a constant flow of miracles! How is it, then, that you still harbor the fear that I might abandon or betray you?

Child, as I have told you before, that thought never crosses My mind—not until you bring it up on occasions. When you trot that wretched nonsense before Me, I will admit, I grieve. I sorrow—especially for you. Have I loved you so long, yet you know Me so little?

Repentance acknowledged. Now forgive yourself!

Forever in joy,

Your devoted Abba

Cherished Child,

Some people become so proficient at shielding and protecting themselves that they imprison themselves in their armor. Sad isn't it?

Mentally rehearsing what you should have said and what you should have done... Talk about an exercise in futility! And please, don't bother refreshing My memory of any sin already forgiven. I engineered your escape. Why aren't you rejoicing? Pull your mind into the present.

With Love everlasting,

Abba

Day 350

Pressured Conqueror,

Don't let the "facts" deceive you. Those facts that your limited mind can perceive are only bits and pieces. The truth, the ultimate and total reality, is too vast for your physical brain to compute, little one. It is so important that you learn to follow My Spirit and not rely solely on your natural reasoning.

At the moment I AM allowing you to face many issues in order to train you to trust My still, small voice. I know your circumstances are hard. I understand that you wrestle with difficult choices. I AM aware of the pressures that weigh you down. I have also chuckled as I have watched you daydreaming and devising ingenious routes of escape. No doubt about it, you do concoct some interesting plans!

Why are you afraid to trust My anointing? What makes you so sure of your own rational processes? Do the factors in this situation *really* furnish you with sufficient data to justify your conclusions? Beware of good ideas. Ishmael was a good idea. King Saul had many good ideas.

You need more than common sense today—and every day, for that matter. You need My wisdom! My wisdom boggles the minds of the astute of this world. I empower adolescent poets to topple giants with slingshots. I grant donkeys vision to behold angels and anoint them with astonishing wisdom to prophesy. I once healed a man's leprosy by instructing him to bathe in a river that was by no means pollution-free. I have even been known to rain bread from the open sky!

And I like doing things "backward." For example, I delight to cure blindness by applying mud to the eyes of My patient, so that at first it appears I have rendered him doubly sightless. Nothing pleases Me more than confounding the minds of those who take pride in their own common sense! Thus My wisdom often tends to reveal itself in the far-fetched, the outlandish.

Speaking of the outlandish, who would have ever conceived of My commissioning a fish to carry a gold coin in its mouth for tax time? Is it logical to talk in terms of taking a leisurely stroll *on* the lake? Your Lord viewed such excursions as business as usual. And His views exactly reflect Mine.

You have asked for My opinion, so here it is. Some of your plans look a little too "logical" for My tastes. Wait for My wisdom! It is My delight to help you! Cutting through mountains of red tape is My specialty. Do you remember how I once freed Paul and Silas from prison? The folks at Philippi of Macedonia talked about that little shakedown for years.

Truly!

Your Dad

Loveable Truth Seeker,

Any representation of Me that makes Me appear less merci-ful and fair-minded than you simply has to be wrong. You know the Truth. Forgive those who perpetuate religious bondage and enjoy your freedom!

In My never-failing Love,

Abba

Delightful Deliverer,

Whatever happened to your sense of humor? I miss your chuckles, your corny wisecracks. I really do. Do you know why I appointed you to this post? I brought you here to act as a "buffer zone" between the bullheaded and the belligerent because I knew you were accustomed to being caught in the middle. In fact, I trained and toughened you all of your life to be the nurturing peacemaker you are. Why? Somebody has to do it. Besides, I know you. You'd be bored with a "normal" environment. If I didn't toss you into trouble you'd go looking for it yourself. I'm sure you won't argue that point!

No, I AM not annoyed. I AM proud of you! You've done a better job than you think. I just want you to recover perspective. Your ministry can be an exhausting enterprise, granted. However, peacemakers like you *are* the ones who will bring about the restoration of all things as My prophets have foretold!

I empower My caught-in-the-middle children to work mightier miracles because they face pressures My other children do not. But you sometimes forget this truth, don't you? I don't mind refreshing your memory and granting you wisdom. I AM your Father, and that is My job. Ask, and you shall receive.

I love seeing you smile.

Your almighty Abba

Distraught Child,

I know your heart. I do understand you. I realize that you yearn above all else to walk in My will—except for those times when you don't! I sent Jesus to heal this schizophrenia common among mortals. Resume walking with Me, and rest in My love.

Dad

Day 354

*Psalm 34:8-10*

Cherished One,

Are you lonely? Depressed? Bored? I think you are. That is why I have maneuvered you into this place to calm and quiet you. Do you think I'm selfish? Some people think so. I just want you to know that I miss you and that it saddens Me to see you struggle alone. Today I want to remind you of how much I love you and of how important you are in My life. You are where you are now for only this reason.

I AM so happy! Now you are Mine—entirely, if but for a moment. And I AM yours, child, just for the asking.

Always,

Dad

Truth Seeker,

Delight in My love and I'll give you your heart's desires. Rest in My embrace. Cease fretting! Trust. Wait patiently. Refuse to return evil for evil.

Trust Me with all your heart. Refuse to rely on your own reasoning. In all your comings and goings enjoy fellowship with Me, and I will direct your steps. Sound familiar?

With joy,

Abba

Weary One,

If you don't mind, we can address what you would like to talk about later. And I promise you, we will! At the moment, however, I would like to talk about thankfulness. I AM so grateful for all your efforts to show it, especially considering all the little shocks that have recently come your way.

I just want to encourage you to remain focused on My faithfulness—not on negative factors or people. As you know, these are destined to change! No, treasured warrior. I AM not being sarcastic. You *have* shown gratitude. I realize that you've not done it with flawless consistency, but you have tried! You need to know that I know that.

You also need to know that your obedience has thrust you into the jet stream of My highest aspirations for you—to say nothing of My promised provision! And I intend to keep you there. Only bear in mind that you should not expect the world to give what it does not possess. Refuse to harbor resentment toward lost people, for that only confirms to the enemy that his tactics to distract you are working. Why give him the satisfaction? Jesus Christ is the Perfect Picture of who I AM. As Perfect Love in human form, He came to show people what I have destined *them* to become.

Child, your fiery trials have caused you to blaze with His light as never before. Are you surprised?

You *do* know Jesus—far better than you think! You've got the picture! Without conscious thought, you show people, you illuminate them to see Who I truly am. Thank you! Keep up the good work!

I'm not asking you to prepare Bible studies. Not that I'm opposed to such endeavors, of course. But you've longed for a return to simplicity, have you not? Now you have it!

Yours forever,
Dad

# Day 357

*John 6:16-21*

Questioning One,

Why do I usually seem to show up at the last minute? You're destined to enjoy servant-hearted rulership with Me in the ages to come. For this, the one character trait you'll need most is endurance. Believe Me!

Dad

## Day 358

Romans 8:35-39;
Second Corinthians 5:14-21

My Treasured Ambassador,

Go! Go in the assurance that I have you covered. Forsake all morbid self-scrutiny. Instead of focusing on your flaws, think of us and choose to relish our relationship. Then it will not be your frailties that others will see. They will see My Light of Life radiating from you—that is, Christ in you, the unfailing Hope of Glory!

I repeat, child, do not fret. It is not going to happen—not ever! I will not let you come to dishonor. Nor will I permit your trust in Me to leave you humiliated and desolate. As you well know, I AM faithful. I may not be predictable, but I AM always reliable. Furthermore, chosen one, My reliability has nothing to do with your track record! It has everything to do with My passionate love for you.

I know rest is hard work for you. At least, at this stage of your life it is. However, it is *only* a stage that you are experiencing, I assure you. Will you believe Me? I AM gently leading you ever upward into imperishable joy. I AM causing you to ascend from one level of glory to another. I AM raising you from one exhilarating height of My splendor to another. You shine with the light of My wisdom, power and mercy. Therefore, your rest *will* come. It must come! After all, it is your inheritance. As you go, you will know!

I have already given you eyes to behold other people as I see them and a heart to love them as I love them. How it delights Me to send you forth to be the blessing I have made you to be!

And just for the record, you are *not* an inconvenience. Almighty God being inconvenienced...hmm, amazing thought, that one! I love your sense of humor.

Dad

ABBA CALLING

405

Restless Child,

I understand. Most church rigmarole bores Me as well. But I AM devoted, incurably devoted, to people. Would you have Me abandon them? What if I made it a policy to abandon you when you fall short of My expectations?

Yours patiently,

Abba

Dear Child,

I AM with you. I confirmed this fact only moments ago. However, your hunch is correct. These days I speak to you less often through other voices. You know why, don't you? I AM helping you to grow up!

As long as you look to others and to the outward appearance of things around you instead of listening to your heart, you will never know the joy of knowing Me literally and personally. A deep undercurrent of restlessness will run inside you. You will not be happy because I created you to commune directly with Me, heart to heart.

But yes. You are on the right track. Furthermore, all is forgiven, just as I have told you, cherished conqueror. I have lavished you with wisdom for all situations. Therefore you are fully equipped for all that lies ahead!

Cease searching for signs and get on with fulfilling your high calling! I have given you many signs. What would you do with more? Carry on! Trust in My integrity. I will keep My promise to direct and protect you. Have I not proven Myself? You know I have.

I AM promoting you—as of today. If I left you in spiritual kindergarten it would reflect poorly on Me. That is, unless I established you there as a teacher. Is that what you want? Now? I think not. I know you better than that!

Yours joyfully,

Dad

Trustworthy Restorer,

Beware of stifling all opposing opinions—even those arriving with blistering bluster! Sometimes one's opponents act as friends by providing a perspective that rescues from ruin. Not all objections imply personal rejection.

Always yours, helpfully,

Dad

Beloved Liberator,

When Heaven's angels heralded My Son's arrival in your world, did they proclaim wrath and destruction on earth and misery for all men? Or did they announce peace on earth and good will to all men? Don't forget! Gospel means "good news."

Christmas is all about Jesus Christ, My Gift to the world. It is about good news of great joy which shall be to all people. Christmas is about peace on earth and Heaven's favor lavished upon everyone, everywhere. It is not about trying to buy love with tinseled packages, cherished one. Thanks for listening and Merry Christmas!

Love always,

Dad

Truth Seeker,

Pursue balance and you'll find only corrupting compromise. Follow Me, and I will bring you into balance. And just for the record: your questions never annoy Me. I love having you in My life.

Love,

Dad

Tense Conqueror,

At last! Now you are doing the very thing I have longed for you to do. You are taking time for us. Wonderful!

What? You think I pressured you to arrive at this point? Why should I bother, when you are such an expert at pressuring yourself?

Recently one of My sons attended his thirty-year class reunion. There he saw the woman for whom he had sworn years before that he would curl up and die unless I consented to make her his wife. She had grown older than her years, as well as become coarse, sour, cynical—and *loud*. Even worse, throughout the whole evening she showered her gracious and gentle husband with whimsical demands and unkind words.

Was My son ever relieved that I had refused to grant his earlier requests! Would you believe that he is still dogging My tracks and thanking Me? Consider!

I realize that dealing with delays is one of your less developed gifts. And you've guessed it right. These days I AM allowing you to experience delays more often. However, My letting you wait is not to annoy you, chosen one. I AM conditioning you to appreciate My strategies while you enjoy Heaven's serenity. Exciting, isn't it?

Yours with deepest devotion,

Abba

Analyzing Liberator,

To focus on self is to succumb to the tyranny of mind-binding despair. Can hell's reign cause the flower of virtue to flourish? Repent of scorning yourself, and look only to Me. Only Love nurtures hearts into wholeness.

Devoted to you always,

Dad

# Day 366

*Mark 4:35-41;*
*First Corinthians 2:16;*
*Philippians 2:5-13*

Struggling Conqueror,

Again, you must test all things and hold fast to that which is good. Do the thoughts bombarding your mind at this moment enhance your hope in Me? Or do they foster unceasing analysis, confusion, and worry? My dear child, there are many truths. However, My Spirit will not lead you to focus on any truth that does not free you to hope in My power and love. My highest priority is that you live constantly in the mind of Christ—His mentality, His servant-hearted love, His childlike faith, His unshakable serenity.

You have the mind of Christ. My Conquering Son dwells inside you. Decide now to abide in His peace that defies reason and transcends understanding. Mere facts will never free you to relish the abundant life that I have prepared for you. At the end of the day, it isn't what you know that counts. What counts is who you know! Of course, that does not mean I want you to adopt a policy of refusing to deal with the realities of life. What it does mean is that I want you to remember afresh that unfailing Love is the ultimate Reality that governs all other realities. Armed with that knowledge, no fact, however real or true, can erode your joy.

Your Lord once commanded a storm to cease that rose on the Sea of Galilee. The winds were real, the waves were real, the threat was real. It was a "true" storm. It just was not as true as I AM! Your Savior knew that. That is why He could sleep in the back of a small boat that rose and plunged amidst watery wave-mountains while His disciples were frantic. That is exactly how I want you to think, feel, and behave. Any thought that renders that kind of tranquility impossible *does not* come from My Spirit. I appreciate your trust.

Yours with all power, forever,
Dad

## Go In Peace

Daring Deliverer,

Go in peace. Every appointment I have planned for your joy. Every encounter, every transaction, and every move I have foreseen and established for your blessing. And why have I chosen you? Will it satisfy you if I tell you I did it because I wanted to?

I AM in control, so refuse to fear! Your faith will bring its own rewards, and you will lack no good thing; neither will you owe any man anything—except the debt of love.

Truly,

Dad

ABBA CALLING

## About Charles Slagle

Beginning in 1971, Charles Slagle and his wife, Paula, traveled extensively throughout the United States, Latin America, and the United Kingdom. Their passion continues to be the revelation of God's true character. Through word and song, as well as through the prophetic aspect of their ministry, Charles and Paula always endeavor to lead others into a vital relationship with the Heavenly Father and His Son, Jesus Christ. They currently live in Euless, Texas, with their beloved dog, Chelsea.

# DESTINY IMAGE PUBLISHERS, INC.

*"Promoting Inspired Lives."*

## VISIT OUR NEW SITE HOME AT
## WWW.DESTINYIMAGE.COM

---

### FREE SUBSCRIPTION TO DI NEWSLETTER

Receive free unpublished articles by top DI authors, exclusive
discounts, and free downloads from our best and newest books.
**Visit www.destinyimage.com to subscribe.**

---

| | |
|---|---|
| Write to: | Destiny Image |
| | P.O. Box 310 |
| | Shippensburg, PA 17257-0310 |
| Call: | 1-800-722-6774 |
| Email: | orders@destinyimage.com |

For a complete list of our titles or to place an order
online, visit www.destinyimage.com.